ruining it for everybody

also by jim knipfe

ruining it for everybody

JIM KNIPFEL

JEREMY P. TARCHER/PENGUIN

a member of Penguin Group (USA) Inc.

New York 2004

Some names and locations have been changed in order to protect the litigious.

Small portions of this book, albeit in different and sloppier form, have appeared in *New York Press*.

Most Tarcher/Penguin books are available at special quantity discounts for bulk purchase for sales promotions, premiums, fund-raising, and educational needs. Special books or book excerpts also can be created to fit specific needs. For details, write Penguin Group (USA) Inc. Special Markets, 375 Hudson Street, New York, NY 10014.

JEREMY P. TARCHER/PENGUIN
a member of
Penguin Group (USA) Inc.
375 Hudson Street
New York, NY 10014
www.penguin.com

Library of Congress Cataloging-in-Publication Data
Knipfel, Jim, date.
Ruining it for everybody / by Jim Knipfel.
p.   cm.
ISBN 1-58542-337-8
1. Knipfel, Jim.   2. Spiritual biography—United States.   I. Title.
BL73.K64A3   2004   2003068704

204'.092—dc22
[B]

Printed in the United States of America
1   3   5   7   9   10   8   6   4   2

This book is printed on acid-free paper. ∞

Book design by Stephanie Huntwork

For Morgan, with love. Her ideas, inspiration, humor, help—and above all her friendship—make it possible at all.

If there were no ugly feelings, would we be alive?

—The Residents, "Would We Be Alive?"

How, the reasoning goes: how can a man write his life unless he is virtually certain of the hour of his death? A harrowing question. Who knows what Herculean poetic feats might be left to him in perhaps the score of years between a premature apologia and death? Achievements so great as to cancel out the effect of the apologia itself. And if on the other hand nothing at all is accomplished in twenty or thirty stagnant years—how distasteful is anticlimax to the young!

—Thomas Pynchon, *V.*

ruining it for everybody

introduction

Whenever I hear the word "spiritual," I reach for my revolver. So I do my best to avoid people who speak or think in spiritual terms. Folks like that make me a little queasy and nervous. They seem a bit too disconnected, too smug, too naive, too brainwashed, too dull-witted. Still, there's no denying it's something an awful lot of people talk and think about.

Fundamental to any question of the spirit, to my mind at least, is the body we're saddled with. When you get right down to it, it's the body that calls all the shots. It doesn't matter if you're a Muslim extremist, a Buddhist, an Episcopalian, a Moonie, a Satanist, an Amway salesman, whatever your faith—if you have a bad cold, it's going to change the way you look at the world. It's going to become your primary focus for a few days. If you have cancer, or a broken arm, or AIDS, it will color your perspective even more deeply. True "spirituality" is reflected in how you deal with things in the face of unexpected and uncomfortable circumstances, regardless of whatever rule system you might swing about.

Near the end of Part 1 of *1984,* George Orwell describes this much more eloquently than I ever could:

"He thought with a kind of astonishment of the biological uselessness of pain and fear, the treachery of the human body which always freezes into inertia at the moment when a special effort is needed. . . . It struck him that in moments of crisis one is never fighting against an external enemy but always against one's own body. Even now, in spite of the gin, the dull ache in his belly made consecutive thought impossible. And it is the same, he perceived, in all heroic or tragic situations. On the battlefield, in the torture chamber, on a sinking ship, the issues that you are fighting for are always forgotten, because the body swells up until it fills the universe, and even when you are not paralyzed by fright or screaming with pain, life is a moment-to-moment struggle against hunger or cold or sleeplessness, against a sour stomach or an aching tooth."

The human body, see, is an extremely delicate, but at the same time surprisingly resilient machine. Mostly we hear about how delicate we all are, about how the tiniest of viruses can destroy us. But people sometimes forget exactly how much it really takes (a lot!) to actually make one of these damn things stop moving for good.

I've not been real lucky when it comes to bodies. And in an odd, even perverse way, it's turned out for the best, at least in my line of work.

(I detail what follows here simply to save both you and me a little time.

It's all right here in the Introduction so I don't have to go into all these things later, with the understanding that we'll simply accept the following as given.)

I was born with a slow, degenerative eye disease called retinitis pigmentosa, which has left me mostly blind. As I write this, I still have some vision left. At least when the light is right I do. The eyes work better on some days than they do on others. I can still work on a computer, though the font I need to use grows increasingly large. I can still enjoy fine programming on the television, though I miss most of the details. I carry a white cane with me, but I don't use it nearly so often as I should.

My field of vision is extremely small and getting smaller, but on good days—those days when the light is bright but not too bright, when the shadows aren't too deep—I can still see with reasonable clarity within that small space. Colors, shapes, some details. It's sort of like looking through a cardboard toilet-paper roll all the time. On bad days, or indoors in bad light, I can see nothing at all.

On those days when I don't use the cane (most of them), I need to scan the area in front of my feet constantly, back and forth, to make sure that the path is clear. Because my depth perception is nearly nonexistent, I've learned to read shadows and silhouettes to gauge the height of curbs, and whether a figure on the sidewalk in front of me is approaching or walking away (if the figure is growing larger, that means it's approaching).

Through the years, I've also learned to use my hearing—which isn't all it should be after all those nights in punk-rock clubs—to supplement what little I can see. I use the sound of footsteps, voices, and cars to help me navigate down the sidewalk. This works fine to a certain degree, but if things around me get too loud, I get confused and can't focus on those specific sounds that might actually be of some use to me.

All told, you might say that every day is an ongoing phenomenological experiment.

These things help explain why, at some points in this book, I seem to be completely blind, while at others, I seem to be seeing reasonably well. Simply put, sometimes I can see, sometimes I can't, and sometimes I fill in a few details in my imagination.

Failing eyes aside, I was born with twisted legs that required me to wear braces for a while. Saddled with a nasty case of early teen angst at fourteen, I undertook a bumbling, decade-long program to murder myself, without success. In various slapsticky ways, I tried hanging, poison, pills, razors, all sorts of wacky hijinks that left me scarred, but still very much alive. When I was twenty years old, I suffered a severe blow to the skull that left me mildly brain-damaged. The resulting left-temporal-lobe lesion, in later years, would transform me into a half-assed epileptic, which required me to take a handful of pills every day to keep the seizures in check.

My kidneys have failed. My nose has been busted. My stomach's a mess. I don't even want to think about the condition of my liver. I've had a few recurring cysts, some of them—the one on my left ankle at least—as big as an eyeball. Fortunately, most of the cysts can be removed quite nicely in the bathtub—and after a few pulls of Wild Turkey—with a shoe knife.

I even had a pesky case of stigmata once, but only on my right foot (which, I guess, would make it a "stigmatum").

There was a period of a few weeks in January of 1999 when I suffered a few too many non-alcohol-related blackouts than I'm comfortable with. It's not that I'd pass out and fall to the ground; instead, I began losing bits of time. Five minutes here, ten there. As much as forty-five minutes at a stretch. I was still going about my business, it seems—showering, cleaning, buying groceries, riding the subway—but I would have no recollection of these things after I came to.

Two weeks before I sat down to write this, a neurologist, after viewing the results of my latest MRI, informed me that I seemed to have a case of what he called "premature brain atrophy." In layman's terms, it meant that my brain was shrinking at an alarming rate. Not at all unheard of, except that it was something that usually happened to people in their sixties or seventies, not their thirties. The news didn't really surprise me at all, considering, and it may or may not have something to do with the fact that I've been having more trouble walking lately.

Although I no longer have any interest in murdering myself, occasional expressions of "mental illness" do raise their hands. So far as I'm aware, nothing was ever really done about that "mixed personality disorder" I was diagnosed with in 1987. I'm sometimes filled with ridiculous paranoias and unfounded fears. I still have occasional bouts of depression. I hallucinate much too easily—and I rarely hallucinate anything of much interest. One shrink accused me of suffering from "de-realization," and left it at that. (I don't bother much with shrinks anymore.)

I prefer hiding to interacting with most people. I screen my calls, and I disconnected my apartment buzzer years ago.

Rounding out this list of my own personal infirmities (for now at least), I suppose that I tend to drink and smoke too much, I lean toward "clumsy," and, in general, I'm a simpleton.

None of these are things I complain about too much, really. At least I try not to. Oh, sure, they can get in the way occasionally, of course—but, in general, they're things not worth fretting over. They simply are, and as such, they are things to be dealt with as the need arises before setting them aside and moving on.

So where does that leave me when it comes to the issue of trying to write a third memoir?

A few years ago, I was lucky enough to meet one of my favorite novelists, a man named Tito Perdue. The thing about Perdue's novels is that they are more focused on craft and style and language than they are on plot. Perdue, in fact, expressed a real contempt for plot.

"Life is not schematic," he explained to me. "Life is fluid and ambiguous—life doesn't *have* a plot."

I'm certainly with him on that, which is why I'm more than reluctant to talk about the "meaning" of anything I write. To me, the books and stories I've written these past several years are nothing more than thumbnail sketches of a life, parts of a life, and in that what they're "about," really, is just a bunch of stuff that happened.

Still, if I were to step back and look at things on a larger scale, I guess I could, reluctantly, say that to date I've written one memoir about the failures of my body (*Slackjaw*), then another about the failures of my mind (*Quitting the Nairobi Trio*). So what follows? If you cling to tired Western notions of what constitutes a human being, the next logical step would be to consider the failure of my spirit. In spite of the role the body might play (and my queasiness over the term "spirit" itself), failure of the spirit is the most dangerous kind of failure there is, because it involves responsibility and choice. It involves inescapables like regret and guilt, which, in certain doses, can be just as deadly as kidney failure or cancer.

At the same time, however, it might also be the form of failure that's most easily avoided. Whether or not I continue to ruin things for everybody remains to be seen. The decision, to quote *The Day the Earth Stood Still,* rests with me.

JMK, Brooklyn, 2004

7

I n April of 1997, the Red River, fed by the melting snows of an earlier blizzard, rose to fifty-four feet, a full twenty-six feet above flood level. The cold and dirty water raged over the riverbanks with a biblical vengeance, broke the backs of towering manmade dikes, and rolled on to all but erase Grand Forks, North Dakota, the town of my birth.

As the situation became evident, all fifty thousand of Grand Forks' residents were encouraged to evacuate. In the end, all but two thousand did. It's estimated that in the course of only a few days, 90 percent of the city ended up under water. Nearly every single home and business in the area was deluged. Ironically enough, the downtown building that housed the local newspaper was gutted by fire in the midst of all that water.

Evacuees, taking only those things they could carry, fled their homes with little advance warning and found refuge at the nearby Air Force base and in local school auditoriums. They left behind family heirlooms, photographs, all those items that had measured out their lives before the waters began to rise. When it was over, when the Red River crested and the waters began to ebb, the extraordinarily good news was that no one had died.

It's hard for me to say why, exactly, the destruction of Grand Forks affected me the way it did. Every week we read about natural disasters—fires, floods, droughts, tornadoes, hurricanes, and earthquakes—disrupting the lives of a large group of people somewhere in the world. In most cases, we hear about these things and then quickly forget about them as other stories take precedence in the papers and on the television. What's next is always more interesting. But I studied the news coming out of Grand Forks compulsively, tracking it down even as the stories grew smaller and were bumped farther and farther back in the newspapers.

It's not like I remembered the place—my family moved off the air base there before I was a year old. Even while we passed through Grand Forks on summer vacations when I was a kid, I could remember nothing about it— not a building, not a street name, not a landmark of any kind. So why should I give a damn? Floods happen all the time. I didn't know anybody there, and lord knows I had troubles of my own. Yet when the news broke, it left me feeling empty and saddened and frustrated. There was nothing I could do. But what the hell could I have done, anyway? Send some sponges over? Those big ones? Or maybe some of those old punk-band T-shirts I figured I'd never be wearing again?

At the time, I didn't even have any money to send. All I could do was listen to the news, and feel bad about it. I had a difficult time even imagining what the devastation was like, so far away was it from my own experience. I'd seen tornadoes and plenty of blizzards, but no floods. Not bad ones, anyway.

When I talked to my folks about the flood over the phone, I found that they were following the story as closely as I was. They told me that the hospital I'd been born in had been swallowed along with everything else, all the old medical records in the basement destroyed.

My thoughts drifted away, as thoughts will tend to do with distance and unfamiliarity, from the tens of thousands who were now soaked and shivering, wrapped in itchy blankets, sitting on army cots, looking at the prospect of rebuilding their homes and their lives from scratch. I began to focus instead on where I was sitting, in the small Brooklyn apartment I shared with two cats, thousands of books I could no longer read, and a bag of empties dangling from the doorknob, waiting to be taken outside.

It wasn't as if I had lost anything. Nothing tangible, anyway. People had lost family albums and collections of letters their grandparents had written at the turn of the century. One woman, in her panicked escape, had lost the wedding ring her mother had passed down to her. People had lost homes and cars and jobs. My apartment was still safe and dry, and my possessions, though meager, were intact.

After I heard how bad the devastation had been, the only thought that came to mind, callous and selfish as it was, was *the town of my birth is gone.* It struck me that some sort of metaphysical foundation had just been washed from beneath me. I felt as hollow as if one of the volunteers helping clean up the flood's aftermath had scraped my guts out with a shovel. I thought about how my birth certificate, the solid documentary proof that I had ever been born, was now nothing more than another bit of soggy flood refuse.

It was dated 1965, long before things like this were saved on computer databases. It was an actual physical piece of paper, with statistics and official signatures, which proved without question that I had entered the world. And now that original evidence, should I be called upon to produce it for some reason, no longer existed.

Of course there had been subsequent documents—driver's licenses, passports, and the like—but that birth certificate was primary. I knew it didn't really mean anything, but like I said, it was a metaphysical question which, in its metaphysical way, cast me adrift. After so many attempts to physically remove myself from the world, why in the hell was I so concerned about a birth certificate?

W hen I was a youngster, ghostly visitations in my bedroom were fairly common. I would lie in bed, paralyzed with horror, as I watched the shadows skulk about the room. The worst and most persistent visitor I had was the lonesome cowboy, who would stand amongst the toys and books in my closet, strumming an old guitar and singing. I never actually saw him, but I knew he was tall and thin and wore a big white hat and red cowboy shirt.

I would hide under the blanket and shriek for my parents until they dragged themselves out of bed to rescue me. I usually waited for the cowboy to finish his set before I started screaming—which I thought was being overly polite, given that I didn't care much for country music at the time. He showed up every ten days or so over a six-month period. Afterward, I never heard from him again.

I also had to contend with an enormous gray wolf who leapt through my open window a couple of times during the night one summer, but he never stayed for long.

There was also the phantom, who hid in the storage room of the basement and grabbed at my feet whenever I scrambled up the rickety wooden stairs toward the safety of the kitchen. He made regular appearances beginning shortly after our arrival in that house in 1969 until we finally moved out, six years later. Every time I dared to go downstairs by myself, he would slink around the corner in his long gray hooded cape. Like with the cowboy, I never saw his face, just the shadows, but this one never sang. Never made a sound. Just chased me up the stairs, slapping at my ankles with his cold, dead fingers.

Jesus only showed up once. Maybe it was nothing but a dream, but I remember it today with shocking clarity.

It was a late summer night. The sun had long since gone down, but the air was still thick and warm, and I had climbed out of bed to go get a drink of water in the kitchen. I tiptoed past the closet where the cowboy was still making occasional appearances, and I felt in the darkness for the bedroom door that opened onto the hallway. Just before my hand touched the doorknob, the room filled with a brilliant white light. There was no heat, only a cool, intense white light and a slight breeze. I turned around to see what was going on, and there in the middle of my small room, almost obscured by the radiance around him, was Jesus.

He was on the back of a white horse and was holding a sword aloft. He looked young—perhaps in his early twenties—and had long flowing blond hair. He had wings and was wearing a robe of white and gold. Given the wings, he might've only been an angel, but I knew it was Jesus, even though he didn't much look like the picture we had hanging on the wall outside the bathroom.

My room at the time was a tiny one. I was seven and my older sister, Mary, was twelve. So of course I got the smallest room in the one-story duplex, the one farthest away from everybody. I backed up against the door and tried to feel for the knob, looking for an escape, but it was no longer there. The door was smooth and featureless, if it was even a door anymore.

The horse reared up on its hind legs and Jesus waved the sword above his head. Everything was silent, except for the slight *whoosh* of the breeze in my ears.

His appearance did not fill me with a great peace and comfort. My heart did not explode with love for Our Savior. I was scared shitless. Jesus or not, here was a glowing man on horseback waving a sword at me—what was I supposed to think? I believed in Jesus—we were a religious family—but the Lutheran God is a vengeful God. He doesn't show up just to say "Hey" or give you a friendly pat on the back for a job well done. He only shows up if you're in Big Trouble.

I couldn't think of what I might have done that was so bad—I hadn't even reached puberty yet—but from the looks of him, whatever it was, it must've been pretty awful.

I closed my eyes tight, expecting the worst, waiting for that blade to dig into my side or one of the horse's hooves to catch me in the teeth, still hoping with everything I had that he would simply go away and let me get my drink of water. When I opened my eyes again, he was gone. The room was dark once more.

Forgetting all about the water, I ran and jumped for the bed, buried my head under the pillows, and screamed.

"Mom 'n' Dad?! . . . Would You Come In Here? . . . Please?!"

A few minutes later, my mom opened the door, groggy and a little annoyed.

"What was it this time?" she asked. "That cowboy again?"

"Uh-uh," I told her. "Jesus," my voice high and thin, now more afraid of getting scolded for waking her up than I was of the Son of God.

She sat down on the bed next to me and stroked my hair.

"Jesus isn't a scary thing," she said, trying to comfort me. "Jesus is nothing to be afraid of."

"You didn't see him," I told her, near tears. "He had a big sword." I still pronounced the "w" in "sword."

She got me a drink of water and calmed me down, promising that Jesus wasn't going to do anything to hurt me. They said the same thing about the singing cowboy and the basement phantom, too.

"He just sings, is all?" my dad asked when I first told him about the cowboy. "Well, does he sing *badly*?"

They never took the night people seriously. They never took the visit from Jesus very seriously, either. They said very little at all about it after that night. Maybe they were coming to the conclusion that their son was just not right in the head. For the following week, I slept only fitfully, trying to keep my eyes open, trying to keep Jesus from sneaking up on me.

He never tried again, but that one visit planted the seed of something strange in my head.

By the time I was eleven, after we had moved to a new house in the same neighborhood in Green Bay, I had become obsessed with Jesus. Specifically, I became obsessed with the crucifixion. I'm only discovering now how common that was amongst Catholic and Protestant boys. I think it's because the crucifixion was so reminiscent of a scene from a horror movie. First the Romans tortured Jesus and nailed him to a cross, like Peter Cushing might do to a heretic in one of the old Hammer films about the Salem witch trials. Then he rose from the dead and wandered around, letting people stick their fingers in his wounds, like what might happen in one of George Romero's zombie pictures, except that he didn't eat anybody (although they ate him, in a manner of speaking, which sort of counts).

I spent entire summer afternoons poised over books that contained reproductions of paintings of the crucifixion, studying every detail: the nails, the wounds, the amount of blood, the construction of the cross itself, the crown of thorns, the expressions on the faces of the guards and the witnesses.

My mother found this odd and unhealthy.

"It's a beautiful day out," she'd say upon finding me poised over another book of religious paintings. "Why don't you go outside and play or something? Call one of your friends?"

"No, I'm fine, I'm okay," I'd tell her, never raising my eyes from the carnage.

By the time I was thirteen, I had lost interest in the Church, and in religion in general. I was a smarty-pants, I loved science, and religion simply stopped making sense to me. I had started reading Marx and soon thereafter became a happy atheist.

In my teens, when kids are supposed to argue with their parents about curfews, how they're dressed, who their friends are, and whether or not they can borrow the car, the only arguments I had with mine were about politics and religion. They could sometimes grow very loud.

In spite of that, while still in high school I went to a Catholic mass a couple of times in order to see (and hopefully impress) a girl I was interested in. She was a very devout type, and I wanted to show her that I was open-minded about the whole thing. After two visits, I got bored, finally admitted to myself that I wasn't open to the idea at all, and never went back. No matter how cute that girl might've been, pretending to be interested in Catholicism was simply too deep a lie to be worth it. Telling her that I had "found the faith" or been "born again" (or whatever Catholics do) would've meant two things. It would've meant presenting her with an image of myself that wasn't genuine in the least, and it would have required that I maintain the deception for at least a little while, which I wasn't willing to do.

She probably wouldn't have gone out with me, anyway. Nobody else did. Dating had never been one of my more highly developed skills. As a teenager, I was too shy to ask anyone out, and too doubtful of everything to consider the possibility that anyone would ever want to go out with me, anyway. I wasn't attractive or athletic or a snappy dresser. I was scrawny and unkempt. A nerd, a geek, a bookworm, a punk. My glasses were crooked and I had trouble combing my hair. The things I found absolutely hilarious usually left other people (especially the girls) with puzzled, worried looks on their faces. I didn't have many friends, didn't want them really, and those I did have pretty much fit the same above description.

As a result, I had exactly one date in high school. It was in senior year, and we went to see *Gandhi*.

Afterward, the girl who had gone with me—sweet girl, but one of your more sensitive types—didn't think it was funny at all when I explained my frustration with the film. It was insane, I told her, that after seeing Gandhi get shot in the opening scene, I'd be forced to sit through another *three full hours* before I got to see him get shot again.

I'd been a very good youngster. I was polite, well-behaved, got good grades, the rest of it. But something I can't quite put my finger on went wrong in my head during my late adolescence. All I wanted to do was destroy things, offend people, live a life of perpetual chaos.

I took to painting crude pictures and anti-religious punk-rock slogans on the front doors of local fundamentalist churches. (There were lots of them to be found in Green Bay.) I would go out late at night when I knew no one would be around, casually stroll up to the church's front door, whip out a spray can or a large magic marker, do my damage, then casually walk away. A week later, after the door had been repainted, I would do it again. I was never caught.

While I was doing everything in my power, impotent as it was, to destroy religion (or at least annoy it a little bit), I had also undertaken a haphazard program of conscious self-destruction. It might've been a bad case of hormones, or it might've been the Devil himself taking advantage of my newly lost faith.

The first attempt took place in the wintertime, right after school. I'd been depressed for a while, but one day something took that final turn. I was frustrated with my classes, I was tired of being harassed and made fun of, I didn't like the way I looked or walked or felt. I'd had enough of it all.

Both of my parents worked, and I knew it would be a few hours before they got home. After closing the front door behind me, I went up to my room, cranked Wagner's *Tristan und Isolde* on the stereo, and set about trying to *break* myself, somehow. I banged my head as hard as I could against the doorjamb, slammed myself repeatedly against the walls, threw myself down the stairs.

Not surprisingly, none of this foolishness resulted in anything more than a few bruises. I was new to the game still. I knew I wanted to die, but I had no idea how much work it would take.

After an hour or so, I returned to my room, quieter, limping, sore, but feeling somewhat better for at least having made the effort. I turned the volume down on the stereo and set about to do my homework.

In subsequent years, when similar feelings and decisions reappeared, I would attribute them to visitations from Bad Spirits. I didn't really believe there were invisible demonic spirits afoot, but they provided a convenient explanation for why I tried to hurt myself and others.

Not long after starting college, another Bad Spirit arrived, only this one was in undeniably human form. Unlike all those others, he didn't encourage me to hurt myself. Like them, however, he provided a convenient excuse (and plenty of encouragement) as I undertook a life of doing Bad Things.

A tattoo on one of his arms led me to start calling him, simply, "Grinch."

chapter three

I was living in a tiny and squalid apartment in Madison, Wisconsin, where I was studying philosophy at the university. I'd started out studying physics at the University of Chicago, but that didn't really work out, so now it was philosophy at the UW.

Grinch, as it happens, was also studying philosophy. He was a wiry, athletic character with curly, dyed-black hair, a wicked smile, and a slight drawl (which may have been the result of his year in the army). A shared interest in Nietzsche, punk rock, movies, and random destruction led us to become fast friends after only a few days.

Grinch, you see, was a rarity, one of the only true sociopaths I've ever known. He did whatever awful thing came into his mind, and he always got away with it. Together, our goal was to make life a little more unpleasant for whoever happened to be around.

I was a bit frightened of him at first. The first time he showed up at my front door, he was carrying a crowbar. A week later, he gave himself a Travis Bickle mohawk in order to make a proper impression at an appearance then-

President Reagan was making in Milwaukee. He had an arrest record, and he'd done every drug I'd ever heard of. He took things much further and was much more sinister than anyone I'd ever known.

He also had an eerie charisma about him: the hopped-up, electric charisma of a young Crispin Glover. He was a very handsome fellow, despite his black heart, and women always flocked to him. His fearlessness when confronted with anything from drunken frat boys to cops in full riot gear earned him the respect of the men, too.

Although he went to all the protests and often led the charges at the police lines, Grinch, I soon learned, didn't care about a goddamn thing. He just enjoyed the violence of it all.

To top it all off, he was a frighteningly intelligent individual as well. I've always admired intelligence, but in Grinch's case it was nothing short of scary at times, the things he could pull up. He was better read than I was, and, in spite of everything, he took his education very seriously.

In a way, apart from his being pure evil, he was one of those perfect types—handsome, athletic, intelligent. And if it hadn't been for the "evil" business, I would've hated him. As it happened, I was admittedly proud that he'd chosen a twerp like me—a simple Midwestern kid with a bad attitude—to be his partner in crime.

Before meeting him, I was content with petty vandalism and some minor shoplifting. In the first few months after we met, he taught me how to break into buildings, steal for real, drink, and smoke. We smashed a lot of things, from windows to construction equipment. We formed a political party together, and later a band. We sabotaged the campaign of a local gubernatorial candidate for no reason whatsoever, and were (so we read in the papers) investigated by the FBI. He even, one drunken evening, supplied me with a moniker—Slackjaw—that may well follow me for the rest of my days. Over the years, we encouraged each other on to greater and greater heights (or depths) of depraved, antisocial behavior. It could be something as simple as lighting up a big, cheap black cigar in a crowded elevator or a fancy sweater shop, staging an impromptu outdoor concert with our band The Pain Amplifiers at three a.m. on a Wednesday during finals week, getting on a bus with a very large ax we'd found, inciting a riot at a previously peaceful protest, or threatening to set fire to a six-month-old puppy on the steps of the Wisconsin State Capitol. We even got the local punk-rock kids to reject us, which was something we didn't think was possible. Grinch taught me the wonder, value, and sheer joy of sociopathology. Whatever we felt like doing, we did.

As we were both philosophy majors, we found it very easy to justify whatever actions we took at the time. We could even cite textual references, the way any serious academic might.

"Here is a course of action," a Frenchman named Lyotard wrote in a book I often carried with me. "Harden, worsen, accelerate decadence. Adopt the perspective of active nihilism, exceed the mere recognition—be it depressive or admiring—of the destruction of all values."

There you have it. That became our creed, and we followed it to the letter.

Grinch was clearly feeding something in me that had already been there long before I met him. For me, the question has long been "Where did it come from?" My parents were kind and loving. I grew up in a stable middle-class household in a quiet part of a small city in Wisconsin. I had nothing to complain about. So what the hell?

Maybe part of it was Grandpa Roscoe working through me.

When I was about twelve or thirteen, my dad commented one afternoon that I had a lot of my grandpa Roscoe in me. At the time, it wasn't clear what he meant. I don't remember Roscoe, who died when I was very young. The only evidence that I had met him at all exists in the form of a single family photograph. Roscoe was an enormous man, with thinning hair, horn-rimmed glasses, and suspenders. In the picture, he's seated in an easy chair. I was perhaps six months old, my eyes wide and confused as I perched there on his ample right leg. Over the years, I'd heard only a couple of stories about him.

In the first, he caught my dad—then nine or ten—sneaking a plug of chewing tobacco behind the barn on the family farm. When Roscoe walked around the corner, my dad was sure he was in for it.

"Hey, that stuff's pretty good, ain't it?" Grandpa Roscoe asked my dad.

"Oh, *yeah!*" my dad replied happily, still chawing away, relieved that he wasn't about to receive the whupping he'd expected.

"You know what you do with it now, don't you?" Roscoe asked him.

"Uh-uh."

"You *swallow* it."

My dad ended up in bed for two weeks, he told me, as sick as he'd ever been in his life. But he never touched tobacco in any form ever again.

My favorite Roscoe story, however, concerns his troubles with the State.

After selling the family farm in northwestern Wisconsin, Roscoe became an electrician. He never studied to become one, just taught himself through trial and error. He was good at that sort of thing. So good, in fact, that he was an inventor, too, designing and building new pieces of machinery as he needed them.

In order to get to work in Hudson every morning from the family house in Hammond, he had to drive his Model A across the covered bridge that spanned the small Hudson River.

One day, without anyone asking Roscoe what he thought, it was determined that everyone who wanted to cross the bridge now had to pay a nickel toll.

Roscoe thought this was asinine. He'd been crossing that bridge every day for years free of charge, and now they wanted him to pay a nickel?

Well, *fine* then. He'd pay the damn nickel—but on his own terms.

He set off to work the next morning with a nickel for the toll, a pair of pliers, and a lighter.

As he approached the bridge, he picked up the nickel with the pliers, and, using the lighter, heated it until it glowed. Then, as he passed the toll collector, he quite casually dropped the near-molten coin into the poor schlub's outstretched hand.

After three days, the toll collector came to recognize my grandpa's car, and he waved him on across.

I didn't see the connection when my dad first mentioned that I had a bit of Roscoe in me, but I saw it later—with one minor difference. Roscoe's pranks, cruel as they might've been by current standards (they'd probably get him arrested today), were pulled for a reason and to make a point. A point, mind you, that he usually got across very well. That's more than I could say. The pranks and petty crimes Grinch and I pulled off were done in true nihilist fashion—for no purpose at all, and with no goal in mind. They were just something to do because we were bored.

Thinking back on it now, it surprises me that, given everything else that we did, we never considered murdering someone for the hell of it, Leopold-and-Loeb–style. We never discussed it seriously, anyway. The idea came up in conversation, we joked about it, but we never sat down and considered any concrete plans toward that end. Still, a few of the things we did stepped well beyond what you'd consider a "simple prank." Lighting up cigars where we weren't supposed to is one thing, but some of our boredom-killers were a bit more extreme than that.

Grinch called me early one night in November during our senior year. His voice quavered with a mixture of rage and joy. *"I wanna do it,"* he announced when I picked up the phone. *"I'm gonna do it—I wanna burn it down."*

27

This wasn't just another one of Grinch's whims, not another project to get rid of the boredom for a few hours. This time They had turned him down again. It didn't matter who They were, really, or why They'd turned him down, or from what. The only thing that mattered was that They had turned him down. That was reason enough. As if we needed a reason at all.

"I wanna burn that motherfucker to the ground," he repeated.

There was something so innocent and honest about it that I found very difficult to resist. He was like a child. A wicked and sadistic child, sure, a child of Satan like you see in the movies, but a child nonetheless.

"Okay," I told him. "What do you want me to bring? And where should I meet you?"

It was that simple. There were no questions, no moral dilemmas. Just what and where. Grinch wants to burn down some building somewhere for some unknown reason? Count me in. That was the way I thought and dealt with the world in those simpler, action-packed days. It was perhaps odd not to encounter any moral dilemmas when it came to something like arson (or anything else we did) given that we were both philosophy majors, but that's the way it was. We'd ended up happily rejecting everything. The only value we clung to was annihilation.

"Come over here," Grinch said. "Bring matches, a nail, and a hammer, if you have one. If you don't, I could probably dig one up over here."

"Yeah, I have a hammer."

"Great. See you in about half an hour. Let's rock 'n' roll."

I'd been a petty criminal and vandal for a while, but no arsonist. Although I'd never admit it to him or myself, I hung up the phone a bit uneasy by this sudden escalation, the potential for serious jail time, as well as the potential for serious injury or death. I was also frightened by the strange new voice that was coming out of Grinch's mouth. It was open and childlike, yes, but it was also cold and lifeless. I tried to put it out of my head. Grinch could be scary as hell sometimes, but when he got that way, I always knew something interesting would come of it.

The nail was no problem, the matches were in my desk, and the hammer was under the kitchen sink. It had been a gift from my father, in the hope that I might become handy with it someday.

Everything fit easily into the pockets of my trench coat. I considered rigging up a sling inside the coat like Raskolnikov, but the minutes were slipping away. It was time to leave.

Was that everything he wanted? Yeah.

What in the hell was I doing?

("I went down, down, down—and the flames went higher . . .")

I stepped out that early winter evening into the first drowning snow of the season, still young enough to believe that I could set the world on fire. Which is basically what I intended to do that night—or at least assist in doing.

The building that Grinch shared with some twenty others was a short walk from my dark, fetid apartment. The snow that night was wet and slippery, and the streetlights glowing off the flying snow cast a strange orange glow over the neighborhood like it was on fire already.

My initial fears and misgivings had all but vanished. I no longer worried that what we were about to do was deadly. Illegal? Yes, but that didn't matter. Wrong? Nope. Deadly? Not a big concern.

The hammer and nail remained a curiosity. The matches were obvious enough. But the hammer and a single nail? What the hell were they all about? The question brought me halfway to my destination. What, were they some kind of primitive timing mechanism? Were they going to get us into the building? Would they be our alibi later, somehow, when we were stopped and questioned?

Slipping down the sloped driveway, trying at once to avoid the parked cars while grabbing onto them for support, I eventually reached the unlit front porch of the decaying three-story student co-op he shared, ironically enough, with two dozen hippies. Inside, the building always smelled like rotting fish and burned hair.

Grinch was waiting for me just inside the door, grinning like a skull. Things, I had to admit, had been pretty boring of late.

"You got everything?" he asked.

I pulled the matches from my right coat pocket.

"Matches."

From the left, I pulled the nail.

"Nail."

And, again from the right, the hammer.

"Hammer."

"Great."

"What are these for, anyway?"

"What, the matches?"

"Don't be stupid."

"Oh—the hammer and nail?—they'll get us into the building."

I was right. At least one of my guesses was.

"Okay, so, how?"

"Break a window. Hammer and nail will do it silently, if it's done right. At least it works that way on cars. We'll crack a window on one of the doors, reach in, and unlock it. Easy as shit."

The smile left Grinch's face as his gaze drifted down to my feet.

"The boot," he said.

"Pardon?"

"It's snowing."

He was right. Only then did it hit me. *Shit*. Snow. Tracks. I was in the habit those days of wearing one sneaker and one combat boot. I'm not sure why I did that, either. A punk-rock thing, I'm guessing. But wearing them tonight ensured that we would be caught, tried, convicted, and hanged all on account of the clear and distinct tracks left in the clean, fresh snow by the goddamned boot. It would give us away as quickly and easily as if we simply stood next to the burning building with our marshmallows and hot dogs, chuckling knowingly to ourselves when the fire trucks arrived.

"Oh, fuck. Well, what's to be done?"

Maybe it had been unconscious. I admit that despite my efforts to ignore it, the prospect of committing a major felony still left me feeling slightly uneasy, but I was still willing to go through with it.

Maybe.

As things stood now, however, we didn't dare make a move out of the house.

"Listen," I told him, "it's simple. We'll just stop back at my place, and I'll put on the other shoe or the other boot. Whichever. See? No problem."

"No, I have a better idea," he said, still frowning. "Let's go downstairs."

In the basement, he rummaged through a box of discarded clothing and pulled out two pairs of enormous wool socks.

"Try these on over your shoes. They'll distort the tracks enough to make identification and following the path impossible."

But try as I might, even with Grinch's help, I couldn't force the wool around the unyielding leather boot. It wouldn't work. I needed to replace one of the two.

"No, I think I have another idea," Grinch said, as he tossed the socks back in the box. "Do you have a *third* pair of shoes at your apartment? One you can get rid of?"

"Nope, uh-uh, this is it."

"Hmm . . . that's okay. We'll be able to scrounge one up around here some-place." Then he thought a second. "No, two more. Yeah. Now what we need is an inflammable liquid. And I know just where to look."

For some reason, I wasn't terribly surprised. I followed him deeper still into the gray, oil-smeared bowels of the house, down a creaking flight of wooden steps into a filthy, cold sub-basement. Grinch clicked on a single bare lightbulb dangling from the ceiling, forced open a metal door, and descended a few steps even deeper into the earth, where he flicked on a dusty 60-watt bulb, also bare and cold.

It was a fireman's nightmare, or wet dream. In the cramped cement cubicle that was the sub-sub-basement, the walls covered with painted hippie nonsense (daisies and peace signs and slogans about the Sandinistas), were chemicals in dozens of containers of various sizes and colors. The shadows from the dirty lightbulb made them seem even more malevolent. Paints, paint thinner, oil, gasoline—mixed together on the shelves with cracked wooden boards and piled with soot-black rags. To sneeze incorrectly in this room would mean instant immolation.

Grinch glanced around quickly, giving the impression that he knew exactly what he was looking for.

"Here we go."

He pushed aside a collection of spray cans and paint-spattered bottles covered with warnings and pulled a large, square aluminum can of kerosene from the back of one of the shelves.

Screwing off the cap and setting it behind him, he spilled a tiny pool of clear liquid onto the concrete floor.

"Gimme a match."

"*Pardon?*"

"We have to see if it'll burn."

"Grinch, Christ, it's *kerosene*—of *course* it'll burn."

Much of the time, Grinch simply didn't listen to what anyone else had to say. It was a spooky, almost enviable, infinitely frustrating quality of his. He simply didn't hear when he chose not to. He gave absolutely no response to my observation as he stood there, looking at the kerosene and holding out his hand, waiting for the matches. I reluctantly handed them over.

He pulled one of the matches from the pack and struck it.

"Stand back."

I was already poised to run.

When the match hit the kerosene, the tiny, clear pool erupted into a ball of white, sharp flame.

Grinch cackled and whooped, hopping up and down and clapping his hands like a child with a happy new toy.

"Quick, let's put this out and get to work."

Grinch batted at the bonfire with his coat, and I slapped at it with a board. We quickly squashed our tiny industrial inferno, then looked at each other, an undeniable, unrefusable flicker of joy in our eyes, the grins returning to both of our faces.

"Let's do it."

I nodded, and we took the can of kerosene back up two levels, to the basement. I still wasn't sure why we were doing this exactly. What he'd been turned down from, why They turned him down—even who They were. I didn't even know what we were going to burn down yet. All those facts would come in time, I figured—but the deeper I got into it, the less it mattered.

After a few minutes of scrounging, Grinch acquired two pairs of discarded shoes.

"Here, try these on."

As I tried to force them onto my protesting feet, I looked up and asked, "So, what's the plan?"

"Okay. It's snowing, so the tracks are going to be a big problem. We'll carry these shoes along with the rest of the stuff in your backpack."

"I didn't bring my backpack."

"Then we'll use *my* backpack. On the way there, we'll take heavily traveled roads and walk in the streets whenever possible. We'll go inside and all around as many buildings as we can. Same thing on the way back, just in case they try to use dogs to track us. We'll fuck them up by doubling around and confusing the scent as much as possible. We'll stop in the library, or some building near East Hall and change shoes, leaving the old set there. Then we go on to the building itself. "

"Uh-huh?"

"When we get there, we use the nail to break one of the windows in one of the back doors, and let ourselves in. Once we're in, and once we're sure that there are no janitors around, we find the office of one Mr. Andrew Hansford. It's on the second floor near the steps. Fuckin' *asshole*. We splash the holy water around his doorway, making sure that the frame, paneling, and nice, polished oak floor are all soaked good. We start another bonfire and get the hell out of there. It's that simple."

He always said that.

"We wander around a bit afterward, then go back and change our shoes again, split up, throw these shoes away in different garbage cans, go home, and read about ourselves in tomorrow's paper."

Then the full story came out. Grinch was set to graduate the following month, same way I was. But he had discovered only that afternoon that a university administrator named Andrew Hansford—the man in charge of such things—had decided that a two-credit art course Grinch was taking could not count toward his graduation requirements. As a result, he was left one credit shy, and because of this, he would need to spend another full semester in school to make up for it.

That's why we were going to burn down the administration building.

By this time, I was starting to worry again. Grinch's eyes had gone to ice, his speech had slipped into a very methodical, unquavering monotone. We were going to do it. We were going to burn a building down. This wasn't gluing locks shut anymore, or dumping newspaper boxes in the lake, or making crank calls. This was something that could get us sent away for a long, long time.

Even though I never thought that I had much of a future—any future at all, really—this could mean throwing whatever there was of it away. Once again, I felt a small flash of fear. This was getting out of hand.

"Hey, Grinch . . ."

"Hmm?"

He was busy stuffing things into the nylon backpack: the kerosene, the shoes, the matches. I kept the hammer and nail in my coat pocket.

"Grinch, look. Everything is working against us tonight. It's snowing, which means we'll leave fresh tracks. The hill will be covered with people tonight. Any one of them could point us out. We can't afford to make any mistakes. So why don't we wait a day and plan this thing out more carefully? Cover ourselves better? We can't afford to fuck everything up right now."

Grinch just kept packing, thinking about what I just said—if he'd heard me at all.

"Look," he said at last, "there's nothing to worry about. If it keeps snowing this hard, our tracks will be covered by morning. The shoe switching should take care of that, anyway. Because there are people swarming all over the hill by the building, it'll be easier to blend in. Hell, if you try to pull something like this at three in the morning, and you're the only one within four blocks of the place when the cops and fire trucks get there, you're dead. They'll just kill you right there. If you think about it, everything's working to our advantage right now. So much so, in fact, that we're almost *obligated* to do this tonight."

You know, he was right.

Grinch zipped up the backpack and flipped it over his shoulder, and we set out to make history.

We followed his plan to the letter: traveled the most-trafficked streets, walked in other people's tracks whenever possible, went into and out of five different buildings—stores, apartment complexes, office buildings—entering and leaving each through different doors, exploring different floors, riding elevators, combing basements.

As expected, there were a few people wandering around in the snow that night. The romantic set. There weren't too many, and they didn't pay any attention to the two who didn't have that wistful spark in their eyes.

Three buildings down the hill from that evening's destination, Grinch pulled me through a shadowed and hidden doorway into a brightly lit hall on the first floor of the music library.

38

Again?

Before we started wandering around the building, Grinch ducked into a stairwell, threw off his backpack, and started to pull off his shoes.

"Get your shoes off."

As I started working the laces, Grinch pulled the pairs of diversionary shoes out of his pack and threw one at my feet. They were tight, but they would do for however long it took to set a building on fire. I took both discarded pairs of shoes and tossed them into the darkness under the stairs.

And that was it. Almost.

For one last time, we wandered quickly, aimlessly, through the nooks and smudged crannies of the building, crawling through as many staircases, elevators, practice rooms, and hallways as we could find. Though we didn't look much like cellists or oboists, nobody would remember us.

We were outside again. It was still snowing thick, wet flakes. Once around the corner of the music library, our goal—Grinch's goal, and what had become my game—slipped into sight: dark, forbidden, inviting warmth.

It was an ugly building, anyway.

We took a quick scan of the environs. Three people were walking down the hill toward us, talking loudly amongst themselves.

". . . yeah, Freud woulda had a field day with that film . . ."

"Yeah, and Christ, all those midgets—I couldn't deal with it . . ."

They passed without noticing us.

When they were gone, we darted back to the most hidden corner of East

Hall. There were four entrances, but only one gave easy access to Hansford's office.

The building was dark. No lights meant no janitors meant no manslaughter charges.

We walked around the building twice, weighing our situation, our choice, our act, before Grinch finally stopped in front of one of the back doors. It was embedded in a concrete-and-brick archway and had a white wooden frame. It was farthest from the light and the witnesses on the hill.

Why were we doing this again? I tried to remember.

"Gimme the hammer and nail. If this works, it should be silent. If not, be ready to move."

He poised the nail at the lower right-hand corner of the window. The hammer was raised just a few scant inches above the nail's head before Grinch struck down sharply.

THUD.

We vanished like shots around the corner of the next building, and ducked behind a set of bushes. We were both trying to swallow our nervous laughter.

"Plexiglas," Grinch whispered, finally. "It must be new. They were expecting us."

"Or someone like us. They certainly fuck up enough lives in there to be ready for something like this."

"Goddammit, we've come this far, and I'm not going to let these bastards off this easily."

"Whaddya mean?"

"C'mon."

I watched for stray pedestrians, government spies, and cops as Grinch unzipped the backpack and pulled out the can of kerosene.

"Here, hold this," he said, handing the limp bag to me. I took it and started fishing around inside for the matches.

Grinch unscrewed the cap off the can and began to splash it on the wooden door and painted frame, even on the brick wall and cement steps. It sparkled under the snowy sky like the purest of fresh rainwater. Clear and sweet.

Though our voices and hands were trembling, our minds were fused into a direct and singular goal: the willful and charitable torching of a public office building, because They (in the form of an administrator I'd never heard of) had turned Grinch down.

"Gimme the matches."

Hands shaking visibly now, I obliged.

("And it burns, burns, burns . . .")

He struck a match that hissed into life and dropped it on the well-soaked step.

The door erupted into a ball of white flame twenty times the size of the one in the basement only an hour earlier. The fire licked up the sides of the building.

Grinch leapt back from his handiwork, whooped with joy once again, then vanished.

The flames transfixed me for a second before I turned to flee with the one person in the world I knew I could trust. Only when I finally turned around did I see that he was already at the bottom of the hill, not slowing down and not looking back, rounding the corner onto Packing Drive and disappearing.

It didn't occur to me until much later that I had been deserted.

I set off like a mad stork down the slick hillside after one last, frenzied look back over my shoulder at the night's work. The fire, though exploding with a stellar brilliance, was already dying away in the winter night air. Kerosene burned very well, but very quickly. Very hot, but very fast. Without a base like Vaseline or Styrofoam to feed it, it wouldn't take, and it would do little damage to the wood, let alone the concrete.

Slipping down the hill, my arms trying vainly to lift me over the hidden flights of steps and tripping branches, I was skiing blindly, laughing like a fool, scared out of my mind, waiting for the certain grip of the policeman to clamp down tight on my right shoulder.

Once I hit the street and heard the traffic and saw thousands of intertwining, intermelting footprints, I realized that everything was going to be all right.

I wandered around in and out of the streets, crossing frequently, doubling back, making and mixing tracks. Eventually I worked my way back to the music library and changed shoes. Grinch's were still there under the steps.

I walked back to my apartment, and along the way, I deposited each of the shoes in a different garbage can (one on the street, one inside a hotel lobby). A smile snuck onto my face.

Now I had a secret.

It was still snowing very hard outside. Heavy, wet flakes of the purest white. The smile grew broader as I got farther away.

At the time, and for many years afterward, I wasn't sure that I'd ever feel that good, that alive again—or if I had the guts to dare try.

chapter four

I graduated the following month, and shortly thereafter moved north to Minneapolis to attend graduate school, where I attempted to fool myself into believing that I really wanted to be a philosophy professor.

The Bad Spirits knew better, providing enough tomfoolery in that unlittered, unworried town to show me otherwise. Even without Grinch around (though he did visit a few times), there was plenty of trouble to be had.

Those Spirits even went so far as to sneak up on me unexpected one night in the middle of my first semester.

I began noticing the pattern again. I was buying all the same groceries at the same time every week. I was walking the same route to grab the same bus every day. Despite my best efforts, I found myself locked in again to a routine that never altered, never shifted. I'd noticed such things before, and every time I did, I knew where it would lead. Even that, in its way, was part of the pattern.

After a few days of consideration, I undertook a comical and ill-conceived attempt to hang myself (while trying to make it look like a murder disguised as a suicide). Failing at that, I washed down a large number of pills with a fifth of bad scotch. I hallucinated (or visited Hell, one of the two) for three days, and came to strapped on a bed in the intensive-care unit of a local hospital. Once conscious, I was informed by my doctors that my kidneys had shut down completely as a result of the overdose, but that I was going to be okay.

What they didn't tell me was that, after spending ten days in the ICU, I would be wheeled into an elevator, then delivered six levels underground, to the floor that housed the locked-door psychiatric ward. They also neglected to mention that I would be spending the next six months there. It wasn't such a bad time, considering everything, though I did question the logic of allowing psychiatric patients to watch professional wrestling on television.

My time in the Bin wasn't dramatic: no altercations with orderlies or altered brain chemistry. But I did leave there vowing (in vain, in retrospect) that I'd never allow myself to slip into the patterns—the daily routines—that had driven me mad in the first place. Life had to change, I told myself; it had to be unpredictable, if it were to be worth anything at all.

I finished up the school year after my release, then on a mutual agreement between myself and the university (they didn't want me there and I didn't want to be there), I moved to Philadelphia with a woman who would become my future ex-wife.

I met Laura shortly before leaving the University of Chicago. She was from Grand Rapids originally, was studying linguistics, and gave tours at Frank Lloyd Wright's Robie House.

It wasn't love at first sight, but we got along—which was more than either one of us could say about our dealings with most people. We stayed in touch after I moved to Madison, then later after I moved to Minneapolis. Over time, and after several visits back and forth, our feelings for each other grew. As it happened, my leaving the graduate program in Minnesota coincided with her leaving Chicago in order to begin graduate school. She was moving to Philadelphia, and I figured Philly was as fine a place as any, considering I had no other plans at the moment.

We found a small apartment in Center City and acquired two cats—a small, evil, black-and-white one, and an enormous, possibly retarded tabby whose heart exploded with love and kindness for all living things. Some time later, Laura and I decided to get married.

While Laura went to class, I looked for work, and eventually found a job at a used-book store. I started drinking more, and my attitude grew progressively worse.

Then one day, for lack of anything better to do, I started writing stories.

One of the earliest steady writing gigs I had there (apart from a column called "Slackjaw" that I was writing for a weekly paper called *The Welcomat*) was with an alternative-music magazine. Each monthly issue was comprised of record reviews, concert reviews, and interviews with rock stars from the goth/industrial scene.

The goth/industrial people didn't interest me in the least, so I instead talked to the musical acts I was listening to at the time—Killdozer, G. G. Allin, David E. Williams, Swans. The editors soon learned that I was also willing to interview musicians who nobody else at the magazine wanted to deal with—so long as I was allowed to do so in my own way.

The assignment editor called one afternoon and asked if I'd be willing to interview John Doe—founding member of the seminal L.A. punk band X— who had just released his first solo record. I told her I'd be happy to, and she gave me the number of the publicist I needed to talk to in order to set things up.

A week later, I went into the interview as cold as I've ever gone into any interview before or since. I had been sent a copy of his new record, but I never listened to it. Apart from a couple of records I hadn't heard in years, I knew little about his previous band, and nothing at all about him personally. All I really knew for sure was that he had a bit part in the Jerry Lee Lewis biopic, *Great Balls of Fire.* At this point—1987, I was twenty-two—I was a kid, a nasty kid, who was a little too sure of his own abilities without any serious justification for feeling that way.

Mr. Doe, when I got him on the telephone, was nice and pleasant as could be. Smart, funny—he talked about his farm, the new record, the origins of some of the songs, and his famous old band.

Meanwhile, I made fun of his album cover. Worse, I accused him of plagiarizing the cover's design from a country-punk musician named Charlie

Pickett. (Mr. Doe said he knew the album, and liked Charlie Pickett, but never considered the similarities until I brought them up.)

I asked boring, pointless questions, which he answered with a thoughtful directness. He was too patient with me, and I mocked him for it. As the interview came to a close, I asked him what disgusted him most in the world these days. When, after a long pause, he answered "greed," I chortled derisively.

After he hung up the phone, I sat down to write an absolutely slanderous story. I called him names, said he was stupid and boring, wondered why anybody would ever be interested in this man's music—even though I'd never heard it.

While there's nothing wrong with being a son of a bitch to someone who deserves it, John Doe did not deserve it. He'd accomplished more than I ever would, and he was still humble and good-humored about it.

I turned the story in to the editor two days later, and they ran it unedited, with pictures and everything, in the following issue.

The day after the magazine hit the newsstands, I found a message on my answering machine—several, actually—from Mr. Doe's publicist, asking that I call her back. At the end of her last message, she said, "And if you're wondering, this *is* about that John Doe story."

Duh, I thought.

Instead of taking responsibility for what I'd done, I called Grinch, who was living in Chicago at the time, and who I knew for a fact had even fewer scruples than I did. We may not have tried to burn down any buildings lately, but a few years after that, living in different cities, we still did what we could to inflict meaningless damage on strangers by whatever means were available.

"Grinch, here's the deal," I told him. "Call this number and tell the woman who answers the phone that you're me. That's all I'm going to say. After that, feel free to do and say what you want. Just be yourself."

He laughed that vicious, dark laugh of his, took the number, and hung up. He knew what was expected of him. Ten minutes later, my phone rang again. It was Grinch, as I expected, and he was laughing so hard I could barely understand what he was saying. The only phrase I caught was ". . . so I said, *'Eeehhh, blow it out yer piss flaps, baby!'*" Then the laughter overtook him again, rolling on for a long, long time.

Clearly, Phase One of my plan had gone off without a hitch.

Phase Two came the next day, when I called Mr. Doe's public-relations woman back and introduced myself.

There was a silence. Then, her voice cold, she asked, "Yes?"

"I'm returning your call?"

"I think you said more than enough yesterday."

"Yesterday? No, ma'am, you must be mistaken. I apologize for not getting back to you before this, but—"

Then I paused for dramatic effect.

"Wait—you said *yesterday*? You got a call from me *yesterday*?"

"I'd think you would remember."

"Ma'am, no—I'm sorry—did . . . did this person who called you . . . was—forgive my language here—but was he a real asshole?"

"That's putting it mildly."

I paused again, then whispered, *"God—it's happening again. Not now. This can't happen now—!"*

Then I hung up, mighty pleased with myself for having made that poor woman's day just a touch creepier.

Two days later, I received another call from the editor at the music magazine, informing me that my services were no longer required—or more specifically, desired—there. And what's more, as a result of my little stunt, the record label that released the John Doe record would no longer allow any of their artists to speak with anyone at the magazine.

At the time, I felt like I had won, that I'd accomplished what I'd set out to do. I wanted to be a monster, a creep, a public asshole. I wanted to do what I could whenever I could to make the world a worse place and spread bad feelings around.

Getting canned from the magazine job didn't mean a damn thing to me—they didn't pay anything, so I wasn't losing any income, and I'd talked to just about all the musical acts I was interested in talking to at the time. What's more, I could now also claim that I'd been fired from a magazine on account of something I wrote.

I bring the story up now because I can't think back on that whole incident (and I do, a couple times a month, on average) without sharp pangs of regret and shame. I still think the post-interview phone prank was pretty funny, but I do feel a great deal of shame for my own arrogance, as well as for what I did to John Doe, who deserved better.

Years after that incident, I finally sat down and listened to that first album of his, and found, much to my embarassment, that I liked it an awful lot.

The question arose: what the fuck had happened? These feelings of regret over some of the things I'd done crept up on me slowly as I grew older and looked back on them. I never mentioned any of this to Grinch, but then again, I don't feel any regret about the things he and I did together. Only when I had been acting alone, when the responsibility was fully mine, does it haunt me.

That John Doe incident, sophomoric as it may seem, was perhaps the first time it ever struck me that I was becoming less interested in being needlessly cruel to people who didn't deserve it. I would soon come to see that I was doing it to people who were much closer to me—not just strangers and public figures, but people I actually knew and cared about.

chapter five

I t's impossible to say exactly when I began looking at some of the things I'd done and continued to do with some regret. I can safely say that it was after Laura and I moved out of Philadelphia and up to Brooklyn in 1990. I wasn't thrilled about the idea of moving to New York, but she was transferring from the University of Pennsylvania to CUNY in order to finish up her Ph.D., so there wasn't much question about my coming along.

My time in Philadelphia fed and nurtured the creature I had first become in Madison. Philly in the late 1980s was one of the worst places on Earth— far worse than New York could ever dream of being. New York, at least, had a few picturesque neighborhoods and lovely parks. The very atmosphere of Philly at the time was one of palpable hatred. Wherever you went in town, people were arguing, screaming threats at passers-by, firing guns randomly into crowds, murdering each other. I watched as people leapt from fifth-floor windows, and as others got dragged out of rivers three days too late.

It was this hatred, this all-consuming vileness, that I fed on and poured into my weekly newspaper column. Everything I did in Philly was done with an eye toward gathering material—some ugly experience that would appear in the next week's issue. Because of this, and because of the amount I was drinking, most of the three and a half years I spent in Philadelphia are kind of blurry today. I can remember scenes, instances, like dozens of individual movie frames, but I have no idea how they were pieced together originally, even what order they came in.

Also complicating my time in Philly was the first appearance of the seizures. By 1990, shortly before moving north, I was having three or four seizures a day, some more than a half-hour long. It was as if all the hate and bile I was sucking up around me and spitting back out in newsprint had somehow become a physical part of me—an extra, aberrant nodule in my brain.

Moving into a small apartment in Brooklyn with Laura changed little. I was taking medication to calm the seizures, but I hadn't quite found the proper dosage yet. I also couldn't find work of any kind for close to a year. My drinking, which had been bad in Philly, increased to levels you might call "merely ridiculous."

The things I found so easy and fun to do in Madison and Minneapolis—the thievery and the vandalism—were all but out of the question in New York, where there were actual potential repercussions to consider. Not only was my dexterity not what it used to be, but security measures were much tighter than I'd been accustomed to, which greatly increased the odds of getting caught. I wasn't in the mood for that. Mostly I stayed home and drank.

Not always, though. Sometimes I got out. Getting out was good.

Two days after I first moved to Brooklyn in the early autumn of 1990, two-thirds of the boxes still unopened, the bed still folded up in the middle of the room, the matters of electricity and telephone service still in question, I put on my shoes and coat, stepped outside, and locked the door behind me. Laura was in class, so I had the day to myself. I figured some exploring was in order.

Screw the Statue of Liberty, and the Empire State Building, and Central Park. As for Times Square (which at the time was still the living, breathing capital of New York vice), I'd get there soon enough.

I had only visited New York a few brief times while living in Philadelphia, and I knew precious little about it. There were, however, a few reasons I specifically wanted to live in Brooklyn when I moved to town. From everything I'd read and everything I'd seen, Brooklyn seemed much more *real* than Manhattan. Manhattan, I believed, was full of phonies and assholes, people who were more concerned with clothes and status and money than anything else. Brooklynites seemed more practical, more down-to-earth, tougher. Brooklyn itself seemed livelier, more of an action spot. Plus it had that literary history, too, and that attracted me. As it turned out, the apartment I moved into was just a few blocks down the street from the house Henry Miller moved into after his first marriage—the same house in which much of *Tropic of Capricorn* occurs.

There was another reason I wanted to move to Brooklyn, too, so on that early morning in September, I made a pilgrimage to the one that was at the top of the list.

From the apartment, I walked up to Seventh Avenue and over to the subway station at Ninth Street. I went underground, bought a couple of tokens, and waited for a downtown train. I wasn't sure how long the ride would be, but I didn't much care, as I had nothing else to do that day except unpack. I sat on the train until it reached the end of the line. Nobody bothered me.

Once I stepped off the train, I wasn't sure where to go. The station I found myself in was huge and dark, and stank of urine. Even though the sun was shining outside, inside I could hear water dripping into growing puddles. I didn't see any signs pointing me in the right direction. I wandered in the darkness and through the puddles, maybe even in circles, until I found an exit.

I stepped out into the sunlight again, finally, but still had no idea what to look for or where to go. I started walking in a random direction, but soon found that I seemed to be in the borderlands between an almost suburban neighborhood and a blasted industrial wasteland. Neither was what I had been hoping to find.

I changed direction, headed back toward where I heard more traffic, and found myself on a grim commercial strip lined with Russian-owned junk shops. I could smell that I was getting closer.

I took another random turn and walked down the middle of a wide, deserted street. Chain-link fences topped with razor wire rose ten feet on either side of me. The sun was out, but the early autumn day was cool and breezy.

In front of me, beyond where the road seemed to end, I could see . . . Nothing. It was as if the world ceased to exist a hundred yards from where I stood. I continued in that direction.

To my right, in a desolate parking lot, yellow-and-black bumblebees with bulging eyes and smiling faces sat in a silent circle. It was a kiddie ride of some kind, but not something anyone would line up to get on. The paint on the bees' faces was chipped, giving them a malevolent, leering quality. I heard a growling to my left. When I turned to look, three Dobermans behind the fence across the street began snarling and barking, squeezing their muzzles through the holes in the fence. I took a few steps closer to them, but stayed out of reach. This only provoked them further. They began to foam and rage and throw themselves against the fence, their yellow teeth snapping at air.

I continued walking down the empty street toward the great Nothing in front of me, the breeze tugging at my hat and trench coat. I turned my back to the wind momentarily and lit a cigarette.

Twenty yards farther, I glanced over to my left once more to see if the dogs were still tracking me, and stopped. The dogs had apparently lost interest, but the cigarette fell from my trembling fingers as my eyes slowly climbed up the façade of the dark building before which I now stood.

The black paint was peeling as badly as it had been on the bees. But this was no amusement-park kiddie bee ride.

Against the black background were images of flames, and spiders, and giant eyeballs skewered on stakes. Hanging from the top of the façade was a sculpture of a great, scaly, winged demon easily fifteen feet tall. He was scowling down at me, pitchfork in one fist. And directly above the doorway over which he hung was the legend, hand-painted in crude gothic script:

𝔜𝔈 𝔚𝔥𝔒 𝔈𝔫𝔗𝔈ℜ 𝔥𝔈ℜ𝔈, 𝔄𝔅𝔄𝔫𝔇𝔒𝔫 𝔄𝔩𝔩 𝔥𝔒𝔭𝔈.

My heart leapt.

My eyes roved up and down the grim façade, taking in all the details. It seemed too obvious, sure, but in this day and age, there's not much room left for subtlety. I was expecting to find a lot of things down here (junkies and midgets, mostly), but the gates of Hell weren't among them. I thought those were in Brooklyn Heights, but I guess I shouldn't've been too surprised.

I was still standing in the middle of the street. I glanced back to where I had come from, then up toward the Nothing where I was headed. I was still completely alone, except for the dogs. Apart from the wind, there was no sound.

I continued walking toward the Nothing, and only when I finally reached it did I discover that it wasn't Nothing at all.

The dark waters of the Atlantic stretched over the horizon. Before the water was a wide stretch of gray and empty beach. And before you hit the beach, there was the Boardwalk.

All these years of pining and waiting, and I'd finally made it to the Coney Island Boardwalk. Ever since I was a kid, I'd been fascinated with freak shows, likely because I so often felt like I belonged in one myself. I went to state fairs and carnivals every summer, read and watched whatever I could about the history of sideshows. Everything I read and everything I saw made one thing clear—Coney was king. If you were interested in sideshow culture, Coney Island was the place to be. And now here I was. What's more, I had it all to myself. And even more than that, I'd discovered that the Boardwalk was just a few yards from the entrance to Hell.

It's a strange and contradictory thing: though my belief in a god has long since waned and vanished, I held on to a grudging respect for Satan (at least as a character and a metaphor).

He was always a much more interesting figure. In books, in movies, in paintings, wherever he was portrayed, he always seemed to be having much more fun than God. And taking a look around the world, and at the way things were run, it was much easier to believe that malignant spirits were the ones who were rolling the dice and laying down the cards.

I scanned the Boardwalk in either direction, chose one for no particular reason, and started walking.

The season had ended a few weeks earlier, so nothing was open. The trinket shops, the taffy shops, the food stands, the bars, the rides—everything was boarded up, closed down, or burned out.

This was back before Coney began cleaning itself up some. Like Times Square before Giuliani sold it out to the Disney Corporation, it was still authentically decadent. It was in pieces, falling apart. Exactly as I'd hoped to find it. It was as decrepit as Philadelphia had been, but much more charming. It had an eerie, vaguely threatening quality, but lacked Philly's open hatred. And even if there was no sideshow to be seen that day, I could still feel the spirits of all those sideshows past crowding around me, letting me know that I was one of them.

I took in the sea air and the blight, listened in the wind for the low moans of long-dead blockheads and bearded ladies, refilling myself with a kind of cultural degeneration that always made me feel at home.

I speak of places like Philadelphia in the late 1980s in terms most would consider negative, but that's not the way I saw it. There, and here at Coney, I found a physical, external manifestation of my mindset at the time. Both were exactly what I needed.

Much later that afternoon, I went back to the small apartment I was sharing with Laura and our two cats, feeling good, finally, about having made the move from Philadelphia to Brooklyn, a move I had been extremely hesitant about because it seemed *everybody* moved to New York, always had, and I wasn't interested in doing something everybody else did. Discovering that Coney was just what I hoped it would be dispelled most of my concerns. I wasn't sure about the rest of New York yet, but knowing that Coney Island was in such easy reach comforted me. I knew that I would at least have someplace to hide when the rest of the world began closing in on me.

Two years later, when I sat down with a lawyer to prepare my Last Will and Testament, I didn't much care what happened to any money or property

I might have in my possession at the time of my demise. I suspected it wouldn't be much worth fretting over, anyway. I did have one stipulation, however, that I wanted to get down all legal-like so nobody could deny it when the time came.

"How would you like the body taken care of?" the young lawyer asked me as we sat across the table in the Midtown office, which perched on the thirtieth floor of a glass-and-steel high-rise. I sort of had the impression that I'd been confusing her, at least to a certain degree, all through the afternoon, answering, "I don't much care, ma'am," to most of her questions. I had no intention of stopping the befuddlement now.

"I would like to be cremated, please," I said.

"Okay," she replied, making a small notation on her legal pad. "That's fine."

"And I want my ashes spread at Coney."

"Coney . . . Island?" she looked up over the top of her glasses at me.

"Yes, ma'am." I wasn't smiling. Ash distribution is a serious business. My original plan was simply to have my ashes dumped on the floor or flushed down the toilet of whatever happened to be my home bar at the time, like Murphy at the end of Samuel Beckett's first novel, but everyone I mentioned the plan to told me that it simply wasn't going to happen. Once I'd set foot on Coney, though, there was no question anymore. I knew immediately.

I could sense instantly on my first visit there that it was a place both of great magic and great sadness. It was there that you could find the last remaining vestiges of a world and a culture long gone, and it was that world—full of human oddities, hucksters of all stripes, finger-poppin' mommas—that I loved so much more than the world we were stuck with now. Nowadays, medical science and do-gooders insist on "fixing" the born freaks through surgery, institutions, or drugs—and the hucksters get sued for fraud. In its heyday, Coney represented freedom for everyone, no matter how much money they had. It was an escape from the city. It was a whole world unto itself; it was like no other place on earth. And unlike the corporate amusement parks that would follow it, it was very real. There was never any denying that Coney Island, fun as it was, could be a very, very dangerous place.

A lot of that was still true, for those who, like me, chose to believe it to be true. That's why I wanted my ashes to be strewn about there, though I explained none of this to the lawyer.

"O . . . kayyy," she said quietly, while making another small notation on her legal pad. "Any place in particular at Coney Island?"

I thought for a moment about having them put into a paper sack and thrown through the gates of Hell, thus saving everyone a lot of trouble and effort, but I figured I'd get another look if I suggested that, so instead I just said, "Off the pier." That seemed as reasonable a spot as any, as long as it was done early enough in the morning so as not to interfere with the crab fishermen.

A few weeks later, the will was signed and notarized and stamped and legalized and put away until it was needed.

I returned to Coney as often as I could after that first visit. Sometimes only once a year, sometimes more. Usually by myself, but not always. If someone was visiting New York, that's where I would take them.

Even as I watched Coney clean itself up during its attempted rejuvenation and try, in vain, to put on a respectable sheen and attract a hipper crowd, even as McDonald's appeared on the Boardwalk and the sideshow got bumped around the corner, there was still enough of it left. Old-time freak show impresario Bobby Reynolds was still there with his hundred-pound rat and his two-headed baby. Nathan's was still there. Ruby's Bar still had the scariest bathrooms in all of New York City. (They were less like "bathrooms," really, than Turkish prison cells, with rough stone walls, no lights except that which seeped through the filthy window near the ceiling, and a trough on the floor. The less said about them, the better.)

In the end, no matter what changed down there, how slick it became, and even as my failing eyesight meant that I could see less and less of it each time I visited, to me Coney Island had always been, and will forever remain, the gateway to Hell, with rides.

chapter six

Patterns can be deadly and pernicious. Patterns are traps, they're everywhere around us, sometimes blatant and sometimes disguised, and few of them lead to anything good. They've been plaguing me as long as I can remember, and they continue to do so today.

The last time I'd been released from the nuthouse (after that long stay in Minneapolis), I'd promised myself that I'd never fall into the same patterns that eventually drove me mad and landed me there in the first place. Back then, I'd become too acutely aware of everything I was doing—walking to the bus, putting on my shoes, brushing my teeth. All the banalities of life began to swallow me up as I recognized not only that I was doing them, but doing them in exactly the same way every time, and usually at exactly the same time every day. The only choice I felt I had after noticing this was to stop everything altogether, so I washed down a cupful of pills with a bottle of scotch.

The years that followed the Bin were a blur of alcohol, violence, and squalor as I sped from Minneapolis to Philadelphia to New York, through dim, filthy apartments, jobs and no jobs, bars and a marriage. Every day was a thrill ride. Wherever I was, I was never sure where I'd be an hour later—whether I'd be asleep or in a hospital or curled up on a bathroom floor in a Hoboken tavern.

In the midst of all that, I had never counted on the whole "going blind" business, and as I looked around myself now, I could see that my life had, once again, become nothing but a collection of extremely well orchestrated, timed-to-the-minute schedules. I began to notice every time I tied my shoes or walked the two blocks to the drugstore. Those are very bad things to notice—or at least they were in my case. I knew where it would lead.

I was officially diagnosed with retinitis pigmentosa, RP for short, while still living in Philadelphia. Apart from the night blindness I'd suffered from since I was very young, I hadn't yet noticed any other obvious symptoms—primarily the creeping, inexorable loss of peripheral vision until there's nothing left. Those wouldn't appear for a few years, long after I'd moved to Brooklyn. When these symptoms did appear, they progressed much more quickly than anyone had anticipated.

After the sight began to fade dramatically, I tried to explain to myself that I needed these patterns in order to function. Everything in the apartment had to assume a place from which it could not be moved; otherwise I wouldn't be able to find it when I needed it. I had to ride the subway at specific times, so as to avoid the crowds. I'm nothing but trouble in crowds. I had to get up at the same time every day, had to leave the apartment at the same time, had to eat lunch at the same time. Everything fit together and was connected to everything else. Any attempt to do something out of the ordinary, anything that would break that schedule, would throw the day into a state of free fall. More often than not, it also meant that I would end up being a burden on someone who would have to lead me around.

Sensing this new, hyper-Germanic experiment in scheduling, this strict, grand expansion of Beckett's "Sucking Stones" routine I had slipped into so easily, so quietly again, both at home and at the office where I worked, I knew that something was bound to go wrong.

A long with continuing to write my column, "Slackjaw," for the *New York Press*, a Manhattan-based alternative weekly, I was also hired to be the paper's receptionist. It was a job I was glad to take, after what had been a two-year stretch of gin-drenched unemployment. The job got me out of debt and gave me something to do with my days.

It wasn't a bad job, as jobs go. I was under no dress code, which meant that I could shamble in to work in the morning wearing my T-shirt, army jacket, torn jeans, and the battered old black fedora that never seemed to leave my head. (The fedora, see, along with keeping my increasingly long hair out of my eyes, also worked as a kind of bumper, the wide brim giving me a split-second warning before I walked into another tree or door or wall.)

Also, because the *Press* was known for having a bit of an attitude, I was told from the very beginning that I was not required to be polite to people. It was, in fact, discouraged. As I had honed my "rude bastard" skills so finely over the years, this seemed like a perfect match.

The paper's offices were located on the ninth floor of the Puck Building—an ornate century-old ten-story brownstone two blocks east of Broadway on Manhattan's Lower East Side. My desk had a pleasant view through three tall arched windows. Granted, it was a view of two gas stations on Houston Street, but that was okay. Lots of things happen at gas stations. Long lines of bright yellow cabs either just coming on or just going off shift, fistfights between cab drivers, all sorts of things.

No, actually, come to think of it, that's about all that happened there.

Since the *Press* was of the "alternative" brand of newspaper, a nonstop parade of the wandering insane marched through the office door, all of whom wanted their stories told. They figured if no one else would do it for them, we would, and they were often right. Outlaw bikers, hookers, pimps, paranoids, the drug-addled, Chinese union-busters, the sexually demented, men and women whose lives had been destroyed by government radio waves, drunken pirates, pornographers of every stripe, the proudly mad. All of them demanded to talk to the editor, and all of them needed to get through me to do so.

The same day I started working as a receptionist in May of 1995, a woman named Morgan started working there, too.

Morgan worked in the *Press*'s business department, but part of her job involved filling in for me at the front desk when I stepped out for lunch. That's when she got to deal with the crazies. She also helped me stamp the mail at night, as well as with myriad other tasks around the office.

Morgan had lovely long dark hair, an easy smile, and the palest blue eyes I'd ever seen. She was five years younger than I was, but didn't act it. Her voice was throaty and warm, and the fact that she was smarter than most was obvious to me from the beginning.

I soon discovered that, regardless how quiet she tended to be, she had a twisted sense of humor, liked Captain Beefheart and Mel Brooks, enjoyed the occasional beer, was neither a prude nor a vegetarian, and was the first person in the office to recognize the images on the postcards I'd sloppily taped to the wall behind me.

"Where'd you get those Residents postcards?" she asked on our second or third day at the office.

"Oh . . . ummm," I said, both embarrassed and tickled, "from . . . umm . . . The Residents." I took the fact that she recognized the obscure, anonymous, eyeball-headed band from San Francisco to be a very good sign. It meant she was someone I could talk to, if we could ever find the chance. Work at the office kept us running most of the time.

Laura had moved out of the apartment a few years earlier. As time passed, we found we had less and less to talk about. I didn't understand the work she was doing, and she didn't care much for my stories. She was also fed up with my drinking and my inability to get a job. So one day, without bitterness or acrimony or histrionics, but with the simple, sad agreement that there wasn't anything there anymore, we went our separate ways.

"So," I finally asked Morgan, after returning from lunch one afternoon during our second week there, "what do you do, really?"

"Oh," she said, with a sly, wicked smile, "terrible, *unspeakable* things."

Yes, this was looking better all the time. "No, really," I pressed. "I mean, you don't seem like the type who wants to fill out sales-figure reports and track ads for a living. So what do you do?" Then she smiled shyly, as if no one had asked her that question before.

I wasn't hitting on her—I never did that. After Laura split, I wasn't exactly looking to court anyone. But these things happen, something always comes along when you're *not* looking.

In Morgan I saw someone I thought I might like to know. There are so few people in the world like that—so few I have any interest in talking to or spending any time with—that I figured I should take advantage of the opportunity while I had the chance. I was nevertheless a bit surprised that I'd been so forward.

The next day, she brought me a copy of the comic book she'd written and drawn a few months earlier.

It can be scary when people bring you things they've done—things they want you to read or look at or listen to and comment on. What if what they've done is worthless, embarrassing crap? You don't want to be mean, but at the same time, you don't want to give them any false hopes and aspirations if what they're doing is clearly a mistake. That's even crueler.

This was a slightly different situation. I'd told her that I wanted to see what she'd done, and I did. Sometimes you can tell you won't be disappointed, and in this case, I was right. Her comic was a delight—the illustrations were sharp, subtle, and clean. The stories were dark without being overbearing, and most important, they were funny as hell. I was thrilled, but not at all surprised a few months later when she began providing illustrations for the paper.

She was well read, and could talk about most anything. We liked the same music and movies, and we could make each other laugh. We hated a lot of the same things and people, too—which is often just as important. It was clear in short order that I liked this woman—and more astonishing, she seemed to like me, too.

It might sound odd—or maybe not—but I was extremely happy that Morgan had no idea that I had been writing my column for eight years at that point. In fact, she'd never read it. Most of the people I had come in contact with in recent years were people I'd met as a direct result of the column. Because of that, they had certain expectations about who I was and what I might do. They all expected me to get stupid drunk and start a fight or break something or hurt myself. That they expected such behavior was my own fault; I just didn't like the idea of playing the role of the guy in the column.

To Morgan, I was just the guy who answered the phones. She had no pre-conceived notions, no expectations, and that was a tremendous relief. Other people in the office warned her that I was a raging drunk and a fuck-up, but she decided to make up her own mind.

My thirtieth birthday arrived two weeks after Morgan and I met. I was not yet beyond caring about my own birthday, so after work that night, a few people from the office offered to buy me beers around the corner at Milano's, and I offered to let them.

There was usually a line of men waiting to get into Milano's at eight in the morning when the doors opened. Several of those same men were still there at four the next morning when they were swept back out onto the sidewalk. It was a long and narrow tavern, dark, musty, with a jukebox loaded with Sinatra and Dean Martin. It wasn't always the friendliest bar in the world—sometimes the mood could be downright surly—but that's the way the regulars liked it. I'd spent many happy and lonely evenings there.

By six-thirty, half an hour after we arrived, I found myself kneeling on the floor in the back of the bar, smoke in one hand, beer in the other.

Most of the people who were there knew about my eyesight, and were keeping their own eyes open for a place for me to sit. Halfway through my second beer, a seat finally opened up, and I was led over to it, where I hunkered down to ride out the evening.

Three hours and several pints later, those of us who were left were crowded around a small wooden table, talking, laughing drunkenly. I casually draped an arm around Morgan's shoulder—a move whose boldness surprised me, even in my state—and leaned in close so we could hear each other beneath the din of the bar. It was the first time I had touched her.

Around ten, she led me outside and helped me navigate the two blocks down Houston Street to the subway station.

"You gonna be okay getting home?" she asked, before letting go of my arm.

We still didn't know each other very well at this point, and to be honest, I'd been a little surprised when she offered to help me down the street to the subway. Extremely grateful, but still surprised.

"Oh, hell, yeah," I slurred. "I'll be just fine." I thanked her for her help and went through the turnstile, and she headed back to her apartment, which was only a few blocks away.

Sitting on the train back to Brooklyn, I was feeling pretty sweet, except for a touch of hunger and the fact that I had to piss like a racehorse. The combination of all these things, together with the darkness, kept me a bit off balance. I really had to pee, but I hadn't yet acknowledged the benefits of using a cane. That would come in time. Given that it was only a five-minute walk back to the apartment, I figured everything would be just fine. I'm sometimes stupidly optimistic that way.

All I could see after getting out of the subway were the streetlights, and those appeared like fireflies—mere dots of light in the distance, and of almost no use to me whatsoever. Everything else was black. Fumbling my way down one of the narrower side streets, careening across the sidewalk from apartment gates to the cars along the street and back again, I kept my eyes trained on the tiny, dim lights at the corner forty yards in front of me.

Now, as in most places in New York, the trees that line the sidewalks in my neighborhood are surrounded by nasty shin-high wrought-iron mini-fences; and as I always feared would happen some day, one of them extended a wrought-iron tentacle as I passed and snagged my ankle.

I fell headfirst across that fucking little fence, smacking my ribs on the metal, tearing the flesh from my legs, spilling the rest of myself onto the sidewalk. I lay there for a second, humiliated and concerned only with the fact that my hat had fallen off. The hat rarely came off except for showers and sleep, and when it did, I always needed to know exactly where it was. Given its many uses, I couldn't afford to lose it.

I heard a woman's voice above me: "Hey—hey, are you all right?" She grabbed my arm and started helping me to my feet.

"Sorry about that," I muttered to a woman I'd never see. "I don't see too well." I had no doubt that she wasn't buying that for a minute, especially after catching a whiff of my breath.

"There's no need to apologize for anything—are you gonna be okay?"

"Where's my hat?"

I sensed her bending down to pick it up. She plopped it back on my head.

"Thanks," I said, then turned around in the direction I hoped was the right one, and limped toward the lights again, my bladder at the bursting point, thinking that I really should get over that problem I had with asking people to show me to the bathroom in public places.

I made it to my gate, eventually, and limped up the steps, reaching gingerly in my pocket for the keys, the alcohol finally catching up with me, trying not to put too much more pressure along my midriff.

I slumped against the door and began sorting through my keys. I only had four keys to deal with, but two of them were the same shape and could only be distinguished by a slight variation in color. I was sweating bad and desperate. I slammed what I figured to be the right key into the lock. Nothing. I fumbled with the keys again. Nothing was working, I couldn't see. Christ. I gave up, unzipped, and pissed against my own front door like a miserable bum or an ill-trained dog.

When I was finished, I zipped up and sat down on the top step to try and get myself together. I hadn't felt any pain yet—I just couldn't move very well. I sorted through the keys once more, then closed my eyes and put my head down on my knees, praying that my landlord hadn't seen me (the front door was right outside his bedroom window). He'd had enough trouble with me already, and now that I had a job and could actually cover the rent, I wanted to hang on to this place.

It was only after I got inside and peeled my wet and stinking clothes off that I realized how badly I was bleeding. I had trailed blood from the doorway into the kitchen, then out into the front room.

I decided to worry about it later, and went to bed.

Before Morgan had let me get on the subway, I'd promised her that I'd be "just fine." Of course, given some trips home that I've been through before and since, that one on the night of my thirtieth birthday might well translate into "just fine."

At first, I didn't know how long things with Morgan would last, really, or if anything was "happening" at all. Not being good at this sort of business, I figured I would inevitably do something awful, or say something awful, and that would be that. Until that happened, though . . .

Three years later, Morgan and I were sitting in another bar. By that time we'd been through dozens of bars, hundreds of drunken nights, scuffles and reconciliations, cat traumas, awful movies, restaurants, bands, frustrations, and adventures.

Along the way, I had both done and said some of the awful things I figured I would, because I always did. There were times when I was just plain mean. A few weeks after we started seeing each other, I called her and made a feeble attempt to break things off. I didn't have an excuse for her, nor for myself. I panicked for some reason. I felt myself growing too close to another human being, and so my immediate reaction was to run away and hide. It had been that way with me ever since I was a child. Whenever I found myself developing any kind of friendly connection with someone, something in my head would go *twanng*, and I would immediately begin taking steps to avoid them. It didn't mean I didn't like them (it rarely did). It just meant that I was terrified.

In later months, I abandoned Morgan both on her birthday and on Christmas Eve. I took her ideas, her observations, her jokes, and dropped them into columns as if they were my own—even gong so far as to take credit for them when people brought these points up later. I left my wedding photo hanging on the wall for far too long. I clung to my schedule. I was, no denying it, an Asshole.

Fortunately for me, we were always able to work things out. For some reason, Morgan forgave me, and we moved on. Sometimes it took a little while, but in the end we both realized that we had something unique with each other, something we wouldn't likely find with anyone else, and that the good times far outnumbered the ugly ones.

Now here we were still, and I no longer worried about when things would end.

Morgan could make me laugh harder than anyone else, and made sure the laughter never went away. It was something we'd discussed on several occasions. She was the one who first pointed it out—once the laughter goes, you're done for. Laughter remained the final measurement of spirit. Laughter, even if it didn't incapacitate the demons, at least helped keep them at bay for a while.

Beyond that, as my eyesight continued to deteriorate, she knew instinctively how to help me find my way up steps and down narrow broken sidewalks and through crowds as I clung tightly to her sleeve, head down. On more than one occasion, she'd even chased my ratty old fedora through traffic-filled streets after it had blown off. In quiet, unspoken—as well as obvious—ways, she took very good care of me. She had unearthed all my secrets and understood me well enough that when the insane fears and paranoias overtook me, she could calm me down. She had become, in many ways, my muse. My only hope was that I was able to offer something in return.

Some people found it odd (and sometimes we did, too) that we never moved in together, that we each kept our own apartment—mine in Brooklyn, hers in Manhattan. But despite the inconveniences that came with this, there were very good reasons for it. We each owned a pair of aging cats, and mixing the four of them together in a single apartment seemed to be asking for trouble. What's more, we each knew ourselves well enough and had each been through similar situations to know that sharing a small space with another person might well lead to insurmountable frictions.

I'm not a believer in anything like "fate," but I am a very strong believer in the rule of chance, and the more Morgan and I talked, the more odd coincidences we encountered.

Perhaps the oddest among them was that we had already met each other once, years before. One morning, as we sat outside the office before work, we were talking about different bands we'd seen. As we worked our way back, we discovered that we'd both gone to see the same Pogues concert at the old Ritz in New York. We'd both been near the front of the stage—and what's more, we'd even shared a drink, of sorts. I had gone alone, and smuggled in a wine-skin full of gin (I think it was gin) that I ended up sharing with her, a complete stranger at the time. I'd never done anything like that before. I offered her a drink, and she accepted. It never went any further than that, and afterward we went about our own business.

And now here we were again.

While many of the things I've done in the past may come back to haunt me, this was one of the rare instances when a simple act of willing humanity had returned, not to haunt so much as to just come around for a visit.

"Happy" had for so long been a dirty word to me. A word I always spoke with contempt. I'd firmly believed that if I stopped being miserable, if I no longer had to struggle for every goddamned little thing, I'd lose what little bit of a soul I ever had, and the stories I wrote would start sounding like those gentle, pointless bits of fluff I'd heard on the NPR or seen in the respectable literary magazines. No guts at all to any of them.

It was yet another fear of mine, and not an uncommon one among people who write stories for a living. What happens when things suddenly start going well? What happens to what you do if you quite unexpectedly one day find yourself *happy*?

Fortunately, it was something I wouldn't have to worry about for long.

chapter seven

One Saturday morning during the autumn of 1997, some months after the flood waters in Grand Forks had ebbed, my parents called me from their home in Green Bay. They were both in their sixties, still awfully sharp, and, thankfully, still pretty goofy. After serving in the Air Force for more than two decades, my dad had spent another twenty years as head of security at a local shopping mall and had recently retired. My mom had held a variety of jobs when I was growing up, from crossing guard to accountant, but since the mid-eighties had spent most of her time keeping house, baby-sitting, and calming my dad down when need be.

With my dad's retirement from the mall, they seemed happy to relax together and do a lot of traveling. I still talked to them at least once a week, and usually more than that.

I could tell at once from my dad's excited tone of voice and the way he dragged out his "*hell-lloo*" when I picked up the phone that he had a funny story for me.

"See, we have all these crows in the backyard," he began immediately, which is what he tends to do when the story's an especially good one.

"Good thirty of 'em or so," my mom added from the other extension. "I'm afraid to go out there—it's too much like that Hitchcock movie."

"And they're *big,* too. *Big* crows."

"Big as pheasants," my mom clarified.

"So the other day—this was something—"

"I came home and found this plastic bag in the garage—"

"Your mother had headed over to your sister's in the morning, and I was just coming downstairs to make myself some breakfast. I pull back the curtains on the kitchen windows, and see that there's a fracas going on in the backyard. It took me awhile to see what it was, but the crows were going crazy. And after looking for a second, I saw that they were attacking this rabbit—"

"Oh, my God," I said. I'd had a pet rabbit once. Charlotte was her name, and she'd been a monster—twenty-five pounds of mean-ass bunny—who devoured candy canes and kept dogs out of the yard. To this day, she remains the only rabbit I've ever known who had developed a taste for blood. She was really something, and I loved that damned rabbit a great deal. That's why stories like this always got to me.

"Yeah, it was bad news," my dad continued. "I put on my shoes and went back there to chase them away, but I tell you, by the time I got out there, those damn crows had taken his head clean off."

"Jesus."

"Your father's not kidding, either," my mom said. "They tore that poor little bunny to pieces."

"He put up a good fight for a long time, though. He was a scrapper, that's for damn sure. There was just too many of them, is all. And they just kept coming after him."

"They're back here now again," my mom said. "And you know Janey? Next door?"

"Uh-huh." I'd never met her personally, not that I remembered, but I'd heard the name come up.

"She's got her gun out, and she's starting to pick 'em off."

"Good for her," I said. Wisconsin remained one of the few places left in the country where, even in the quietest and most comfortable of suburbs, you could get away with whipping out your gun and blasting something in your backyard.

"I tell you, with that rabbit, though," my dad said, back to the rabbit again, "you've heard the phrase, 'the fur was flying'? The fur was *everywhere*. He gave it all he could, but it was just too much."

"That's too bad . . . did you have to clean up what was left?"

"Yeah, I just put it into a garbage bag. It's in the garage now," my dad said. "Fortunately, it's cold enough out there that it won't stink so bad."

"Uh-huh." We chatted a bit more. Local news, how my nieces were doing in school, how I was doing at work. Which relatives they'd heard from recently. The weather.

Hours after they hung up, I couldn't shake that story about the rabbit. I tried to imagine the panic he must have felt in those final minutes, knowing he was going to die. Beyond that, though, what bothered me most was envisioning the slow, agonizing torture of having a thousand pecks taken out of his flesh, one after another. One peck was no big deal, I figured. He probably dealt with that on a daily basis. Two or three may smart some, but I assumed they could be shaken off without too much fuss. It's when those sharpened, bone-hard beaks had struck a hundred times. *That's* when you start to worry.

Sometimes you can just tell, and the minute the man shuffled through the front door of the *Press* and started toward me, trapped there behind my receptionist's desk, I could tell.

A month earlier, the *Press* had moved its offices from the Puck building on the Lower East Side to a sterile, featureless fourteenth-floor office in Chelsea, just three blocks south of Madison Square Garden. Most of the office could've been mistaken for the digs of any mid-level insurance company in America, with its olive-drab carpeting, beige walls, and row upon row of cubicles.

The reception area, which was separated from the rest of the office by a locked door, was something else. My desk was positioned behind a very long and very tall counter at one end of an otherwise barren white cube. There were no windows and no view of the gas stations, and most of the human contact I had came in the form of the strangers who stepped through the front door. Like this guy.

I knew I was in for a time. It was something about his scrubby white beard and crusty knit cap, the way he moved within the layers of ancient, soiled coats and scarves that hid his spindly frame. He bore a passing resemblance to Grady from *Sanford and Son*—or Dick Gregory.

He leaned in too close over the top of my desk, and asked, "Denise Carter around?"

I had to think about that one a second. "You mean *Dennis* Carter? No. No, he's not." We had a Dennis, but no Denise.

"No, I mean *Denise*. When's she gonna be in?"

I sighed, closed my eyes, and attempted to maintain my composure before continuing. "First of all, Dennis is a *he,* and I have no idea when or if I expect him today."

"It's Denise."

Peck.

"I know who works here," I told him calmly. Then I pulled out the list of employee phone extensions and pointed. "Here he is. 'Dennis.' See? We don't have a Denise Carter. No Denises at all. Just Dennis. And he has no set schedule. I haven't seen him all week." It was a lie, of course—Dennis was at his desk that very minute, but I knew better. This is what receptionists do.

Only then was I beginning to notice the heavy stench rolling off my visitor.

"Oh," he said. "I read the name too fast. When's he coming in?"

"I don't know," I said.

He replied with the last thing in the world any receptionist wants to hear: "I'll wait for him."

Peck.

"It would be better if you just left him a little note, okay? Here's a piece of paper, and here's a pen." I slapped them on top of the counter that separated us. "You can go over there and write it. I'll pass it along to him."

"It's extremely important."

"I don't doubt it for a minute."

"How can I be sure he'll get it?"

Questions like that always pissed me off.

"I'm a Trained Professional," I assured him. "I'll pass the note along to him. Now just go over there and write it out."

I noticed the quaver in his voice, when on his way over to a chair, he continued talking.

"Things people don't know about," he said, less to me than to the otherwise empty room. "Doctors, hospitals. Things they don't know about it. Medicine . . . Man like me can have a cerebral brain hemorrhage and survive it . . . don't kill him, maybe, but it sure fucks him up bad. Fucks him for *life.*"

Peck, peck.

"Uh-huh," I replied, mildly surprised to have heard the phrase "cerebral brain hemorrhage" come out of his mouth.

He set his bag on the floor and went about the slow, shaky, and painful business of lowering himself into the chair.

"Things going on in this town that people don't know about. City council. We're real close to bein' under fascism."

"Uh-huh." I started back to my regular work, hoping the phone would start ringing off the hook.

Once he was in the chair, he doubled over, pen and paper in hand, and sat perfectly still, composing his thoughts, as his rank odor slowly filled the small, windowless room.

Lisa, one of the editors, came through the front door and I gestured her over.

"Hey, Slacky," she asked. "What's up?"

"Two things," I said. "Remember that you have an interview coming in at three-thirty—and if you see Sam, tell him that the paperwork he was after is in his mailbox. That'd be great."

It was a ruse, of course. There was no interview, and there was no paperwork in Sam's mailbox. But as I spoke, I scribbled Lisa a message on the piece of paper in front of me:

NOT PAID NEARLY ENOUGH.

For the next hour, Denise Carter's friend sat in his chair, scratching out his note on the small piece of paper I'd provided. I never gave people regular-sized sheets of paper to leave notes for absent employees. Small piece of paper, smaller note, usually gets them out of the office faster. It didn't seem to be working very well in this case.

Employees came and left. Most of them glanced at the old man in the chair, then back at me. A few of them had sympathy in their eyes. Most had wicked looks of amusement. It didn't bother me. The bastards would get theirs one day.

When he had finally finished, he hobbled back to the desk and, without a word, gently placed the neatly folded note down in front of me.

Peck, peck, peck.

Then he went back to the chair and lowered himself into it once again.

Oh, Jesus Christ.

I tried to ignore him, but after a few minutes, I heard a noise. I peered over the top of the desk to see that he had hoisted both his pant legs up and was scratching furiously at his scabby calves.

Peck, peck, peck, peck.

I turned back to work, a twist of hopeless disgust on my face. Finally the scratching stopped and I heard a squishy noise, and smelled something that wasn't the thick, noxious stench of sweat, piss, and shit that had distracted me for the previous hour. I peered over the top of the desk again. He had pulled out three bottles of skin ointment and set them on the floor next to his feet. He was slathering his right leg.

Peckpeckpeckpeckpeck . . .

"Aw, Jesus Christ, sir—could you do that someplace else?"

He didn't acknowledge me.

"This is not a public restroom, sir," I said, easily slipping into officious-prick mode. "Please go find one."

No response.

As I watched with a mixture of amazement and horror, he moved from one bottle to the next, to the next, then back to the first one. When he was done greasing up both legs, he put the bottles back in his bag. I looked back to my computer, assuming he was finished now and would be leaving soon. Shortly thereafter, I realized two things. First, I am a very stupid man, and second, the smell of baby powder is unmistakable.

When he was through scratching and flaking and oozing and greasing and powdering, he replaced everything in his bag, stood, and came back over to my desk.

"Big football game, huh?" he announced, in what seemed a stab at normal, commonplace friendliness. "The Jets?"

This time it was my turn not to respond. I picked up the note he'd written and left the room to put it in Dennis's mailbox. Normally, I would read such things after the person left, maybe even make a photocopy if it was funny enough, but this time I didn't care. When I came back to the reception area, he was still waiting.

"People don't know what's goin' on," he said. "They won't be able to stop it."

"I passed your note along to Dennis," I told him, my voice tired. "Maybe he can help you later."

"He coming back today?"

I pointed at the door, and glared at him in silence. At last he took the hint.

After the old man left, I went back to the mailboxes, retrieved the note he had written, and tossed it in the trash. I was afraid that if Dennis saw it—it was a long shot, but the possibility was there—he might decide to do something with it. If he did, that meant I'd have to deal with this man again. I was in no mood.

When you hear people on the train, or when a friend calls you on the telephone, you often know what they're going to say before they say it. Even if you don't know exactly what they'll say, you can usually narrow it down to a few basic things. Some people, however, cannot be predicted that easily. Some are interesting. Some are geniuses, and some are comedians. A good number of them, however, are dangerous and scary. They're the crows you have to watch out for.

I returned to my desk, where the phones started ringing again, and faceless strangers continued to yell at me. That's what most of the calls to the paper involved—people yelling at me.

"Hello, *New York Press*," I always said, in a voice that rested somewhere between a croak and a drone.

"I called earlier about the personal ads," one woman told me, "and they gave me the wrong box number. So I called back and got another number, and *that* one was wrong, too."

I heard that sort of thing several dozen times a day. I explained as gently as possible, "There's no one in that department to help you right now. They'll be back tomorrow morning around nine. Maybe ten." Actually, I never knew when the guy who ran the personals was coming in, and even if he did come to work, there was no guarantee that he'd be taking calls. He rarely did. He didn't like dealing with these people any more than I did.

"What does all this *mean*?" The hysteria was edging into the woman's voice.

"Well, ma'am"—I know how these people could get—"it means that you're going to get stupider, and stupider, and stupider. Much older, too. And then you'll eventually die. Probably alone."

Before leaving each night, my job was to stamp all the mail that had accumulated over the course of the day, stuff it into as many large gray mail sacks as were necessary (usually two or three), drag them out to the sidewalk, and start looking for a mailbox to overload.

Back at the Puck building, this was something Morgan and I had done together. It became a ritual. When the mailbags were empty, the day was officially over, and we could go grab a few beers around the corner.

But Morgan had left the paper shortly before the move uptown, taking a job as an animator. I was sorry to see her leave—she kept me sane behind that desk—but it made sense. The animation job paid much better, and allowed her to do something she loved.

We still got together for a few beers every night, but before I could see her, I still had to do the mail, lock up the office, drag the mailbags downstairs, then tap my way to the subway, which dropped me off a few short blocks from our home bar. We usually arrived within a few minutes of each other.

In her time at the *Press,* she'd dealt with enough assholes on the phone and crazies shambling through the front door to understand what I'd gone through that day, and why it was beginning to get to me.

The bar we were going to at the time was a few doors down from Milano's. We liked it because it was much quieter than Milano's, and the bartender was far less surly. It was as dark and narrow as Milano's—darker and narrower, even—but once we seated ourselves at the bar, we didn't need much else. We had each other to talk to, and the bartender never let our pint glasses get dry.

Sometimes it felt like Morgan and I, from the moment we met, had been having a single conversation, which spanned both several years and hundreds of topics, each flowing into the next. A conversation that was interrupted only by work and sleep.

She taught me more than any university professor ever had, about everything from animation and photography, to biology and chemistry, to computers, music, and New York itself. She'd been born here—one of the few who had—and had her own share of adventures in the years before we met.

Leaving the bar and saying good-bye every night was difficult, but we both had cats that needed feeding, and we both needed to get up for work the next day. And though we were usually pretty soused by the time we parted, I was left with plenty to keep my brain occupied on the way home. Sometimes I just thought about her, and that was even better.

Sometimes, though, no matter how good a time we'd had together, nothing could erase what the day had been, days like the one I'd just been through, and all the similar days that were beginning to gang up on me, and after kissing her good night, I would step aboard a Brooklyn-bound train still feeling beaten, scraped up, and sapped from the office—and drunk on top of it.

I sat down and closed my eyes to block out the external stimuli. After the train jerked out of the station, however, the music erupted directly in front of me. There was no escaping it.

New York offers a remarkable variety of musicians who make the subway rounds—a cappella groups, folk guitarists, singers, one-armed guys who play the harmonica (badly), violinists, clarinetists, and accordionists. Even saw a guy with a tuba once. Some are more talented than you'd expect to find in the subway. Some aren't. Many—though not as many as should—even take to apologizing for their lack of talent before they begin.

I opened my eyes, knowing exactly what I would see: the three-piece mariachi outfit, God bless 'em. A singer shaking a pair of maracas, another playing a concertina, and a third picking nimbly at an enormous Spanish guitar, all three of them dressed like something out of a cartoon—fringed ponchos, sombreros, the works—performing some of the saddest songs I have ever heard. Unfortunately, knowing precious little Spanish, I had no idea what they were singing about. Something awfully sad, though.

Despite everything, the events of the day, my weary drunken state, I smiled, if weakly. I always expected them after days like this. If I left work feeling like my head had been locked in a metal brace before being drilled through a few times with a broken awl, they'd show up, without fail, like my own personal, elusive, ghostly Greek chorus—one whose warnings I would never be able to comprehend or heed.

It wasn't until the third or fourth time they surfaced after remarkably rotten days that I'd come to recognize it as a pattern. I soon came to expect and ache for their appearance, as it would justify what I was feeling. They never showed up at any other time. If the mariachi band showed up, I knew that it had been an evil one.

And here they were again.

They never moved, never strolled up and down the aisle of the train asking for change as they played. No, they stood where they were, planted firmly in front of me, playing their broken hearts out.

Funny, I thought, *I've never seen them actually board the train.*

I let my eyes fall shut again, glad they'd found me once more—and knowing that, because they had, I was doomed.

Things always seemed to get a bit brighter when I finally reached my apartment, closed the door behind me, and was greeted by my two beasts.

They always came out to say hello. They'd both been with me since my earliest days in Philly, they'd seen everything (in their own way), and I loved them much more than I did most people. From their first days together, the enormous, overtoed tabby whose heart was overflowing with goodness had loved the small, tuxedoed evil one with everything he had, and she in turn hated the very fact that he moved and breathed. After thirteen years together, he was still pining and mooning, and she was still hissing whenever he entered a room.

As they grew older, they'd both grown a bit battier. Of late, his pining and mooning had taken the form of obsessive harassment. As she slept, he would creep up beside her and stare. Just stare, purring, down at her curled form, until she woke up and started hissing. It was very odd. Both of them had developed a few quirks like that.

Despite my weariness and drunkenness, they insisted on keeping me up most of that night, yelling at ghosts and banging their heads against window frames. Nothing I did could convince them to do otherwise. *Maybe Jesus has come to see them this time,* I thought at one point, as I struggled to get at least a bit of rest.

After an accumulated three hours of sleep (in ten-minute snatches), I headed in to work already grim and scratchy and limping hard off the left heel, which had been giving me some trouble of late. A small growth of some kind. I had been applying the necrifying agent suggested to me by a doctor weeks earlier, but all that seemed to be doing was dissolving my flesh.

The phone started ringing at work not long after I got settled in, peeled the lid off my coffee, and lit the morning's fourth cigarette. The door to the office across the hallway opened. I was never really sure what went on over there across the hall. Business of some sort. A distinguished old man in a crisp black hat, a tailored black winter coat, and a long snow-white beard stepped out, stopped, and stared through the open doorway at me. There was no one else around.

"It's all your fault," he said, with a cold resolve, and not the slightest hint of a smile.

"I hear that a lot," I told him. "I know . . . and I'm sorry." Then he got on an elevator and disappeared.

It was true. On subways, in diners, on the street, over the phone, once or twice a week, out of the blue, someone, a stranger, would tell me that it was entirely my fault. They rarely shared with me what "it" was, and I knew better than to ask. I'd always assumed it was a joke of frustration until this little old man uttered it with such conviction. He was waggling a thoroughly solemn finger-bone of blame in my direction. Whatever trouble he had found himself embroiled in, he knew that I was its root cause.

It was certainly possible, I suppose. Along with the thing on my heel, in the previous weeks I'd also been plagued by short blackouts. More than I was used to. At one point, I even found myself standing at the top of the subway steps on the corner of Sixth Avenue and Twenty-third Street, struggling (and failing) to light a smoke in a damp wind while trying, for the life of me, to figure out exactly how I'd reached that point. It wasn't a philosophical question this time.

I remembered eating my bowl of cereal and swallowing a mug of cold coffee. I remembered brushing my teeth and taking my anti-convulsive pills. I remembered sitting down on the wooden bench in my kitchen to put on my shoes. But after that, nothing—nothing at all—except that now I was standing on a street corner in Manhattan, surrounded by dark-eyed proles dancing to get around me on their way to work.

I looked at my watch. It was seven thirty-five in the morning. I usually left the house a little before seven. I'd lost close to forty-five minutes.

I didn't remember putting on my coat, locking the apartment door behind me, walking to the train, dropping my token into the slot, waiting on the platform, getting on the train, riding into Manhattan, getting off the train, or climbing the stairs to the street. I don't think I was sleeping through it all. I've never been known to sleepwalk.

I'd been losing minutes here and there in the days prior, but never quite this much at once. I wondered—What have I been doing in those dark times?

What can a man do in forty-five minutes, or fifteen, or five?

Any number of things, if you really think about it. Stealing, of course. That only takes a second if you're good. You could make a whole bunch of telephoned bomb threats. Start a fire and walk away. Stop and slash some car tires on your way down the street. Even kill a man. Only trouble with that would be the problem of hiding the evidence and cleaning yourself up. My

God, had I been hearing news stories over the past weeks about robberies and murders in which the police had no suspects, unaware that I was actually hearing stories about things I had done during these blackouts?

Unless you have someone like a spouse to keep an eye on you as you sleep, how do you really know what you're up to after you lay your head on the pillow and close your eyes at night? Ever wake up the next morning exhausted and not know why? Maybe without realizing it, you're climbing out of bed at night, getting dressed, going out, and releasing all the neighbors' dogs. Or worse, going jogging.

The possibilities are really quite staggering. When my seizures first started getting bad in the late 1980s, I didn't remember a single thing I did or said during those periods—and I did some pretty awful things. I said things I never could have thought, bit myself, put my fist through a bathroom wall. And afterward, had no memory of it at all, except for muscle aches, tooth marks on my arm, or a girlfriend (my future ex-wife) who was extraordinarily pissed. In my own mind, I had done nothing at all. At least nothing I could remember at the moment. Yet to hear it told, I had become Jack Nicholson backing Shelley Duvall up the stairs in *The Shining*.

So, blatant crimes and vicious behavior are the first things that come to my mind when I consider the buried possibilities of these blackouts. Then again, lawyers have certainly tried using blackouts and sleepwalking as defenses in murder cases, usually with pretty miserable results.

Instead of committing crimes, you could just as easily be out there quietly performing good deeds, I suppose—saving kittens, dropping quarters in parking meters and what have you. Other people—people I had met in that reception area, as a matter of fact—would suggest that the lost time was the result of alien abduction. Or the work of electronic mind-control devices employed by secret government agencies.

I know some people who would believe that in those lost minutes they became, perhaps, invisible agents of Satan, minor demons traipsing around on cloven hooves, gray, soiled wings hidden under long black coats, provoking all the minor annoyances that people encounter on a daily basis. Traffic jams, faxes that don't get there, phones calls that arrive or don't arrive, water that doesn't taste right, careers that never quite get off the ground, hangnails, broken marriages, diseases, puddles that are deeper than you expected. All the work of invisible malevolent forces.

I am not clever, imaginative, or arrogant enough to think of myself in such terms. I'm just a simple blind man with a lifelong history of psychological and neurological problems. I know the old man was blaming me for his trouble because, simply enough, there I was, sitting right there. I was an easy target. It was the same as with most everyone on the other end of the phone who tore into me. They didn't know who I was, but goddammit, *there* I was: a receptionist, no one else around to blame, an easy target for a finger-waggling, helpless to confirm or deny my innocence. At least this old man was an equally easy target for me, to provide an explanation for something I hadn't been able, and hadn't needed, to explain.

Despite the visitors with their various ointments, and the irate, slow-witted types who clogged the phone lines, being the paper's receptionist was a good deal of fun for a couple of years. I heard woeful paranoid tales and read cramped, handwritten manifestos before anyone else had the chance. However, with time and a growing weariness—the parade never did stop—my enthusiasm had waned. All the stories were beginning to sound pretty much like all the others, like they were all copped from a single original script. The same was true with my days.

I'd get up, ride the train to work, then talk to insane and angry people for the next ten hours. At the end of the day, I'd drag the mail out to the mailbox a block away, then hide in a bar for a few pleasant and relaxed hours afterward with Morgan. Then I'd go home, pet the cats, eat something, go to bed, get up, and do the same thing the next morning.

After sitting behind that desk for three years, I now found myself tempted to quit on a daily basis, but I had no choice but to hold on to the job. What else could I do? Nobody was going to hire me for anything worthwhile. Experience had taught me that much already. Now that I was losing my sight on top of it, my options were reduced even further.

Jimmy"—Trixie was the only one apart from an ex-cop I knew who called me "Jimmy" without being snide about it—"can I ask you a personal question?"

"Sure," I said. I liked Trixie. She was in her early forties, a tough-as-snot Bronx girl who took no shit, chain-smoked, and drank straight vodka on her lunch break. She'd been working at the paper for about a year, but already I could see it was taking its toll. I was always the first one there in the mornings, she was often the second, and it wasn't uncommon for her to stop by my desk to kvetch a little bit.

"How do you do it? I mean, how do you put up with these people?" she asked, gesturing toward the rest of the otherwise empty office. She asked me that question a lot.

I told her the same thing I told her every time she asked. "I keep my head down and try to keep my big yap shut."

"Yeah, it's like you got some big, weird *bubble* around you or something," she said, putting a cigarette in her mouth and reaching for one of the packs of matches scattered across my desk. "Everyone here is scared to death of you."

"Oh, I don't know about that," I said. I certainly didn't get that impression, anyway. Mostly they just wanted me to overnight packages for them and screen their calls. Apart from that, though, thinking about it, I guess they did keep their distance. That was a relief. Most of the people who worked there were youngsters. I don't have the patience for youngsters.

It's an overworn and tattered cliché, but I've always felt like an old man. When I was a twenty-five-year-old bill collector in Philadelphia, a woman in the office once asked me, "How did a seventy-year-old man end up in your body?" I had no answer for her.

I'd been feeling older than usual in recent years, even at the tender age of thirty-three. At the paper, I was surrounded by kids in their early twenties, some even younger, all full of life and laughter, talking in raised, excited voices about some pop band I'd never heard of or, much more terrifyingly, of some political columnist they liked or despised. They just irked me, these damn kids and this zeal of theirs. They also made me feel a dozen years older than I was. As a result, I had little to say to them. It's a bad scene when you feel old but hardly grown up.

"No—it's true, you scare the shit out of people," Trixie said. "I mean, face it, Jimmy—you're one creepy motherfucker."

She was one of the few people who could say something like that and have it come out sounding like a compliment.

In late 1997, I was contacted by a publisher who was interested in having me write a book. It was an idea I had resisted for a very long time. I was happy with the sheer disposability of newspaper writing. Write a story, it appears in the paper, then it's gone and forgotten a week later. The old nihilist in me found that very attractive. Every week was like starting over, and none of it meant a damn thing.

But after doing that for over a decade, living week to week that way, and getting older at the same time, I began to think that maybe there wasn't anything all that wrong with leaving something a little more solid behind. I agreed, and signed the contract.

A year later, not long before my first book was set to be released, I also decided that I simply could not sit at that reception desk any longer. Problem was, I was never that adept at job-hunting. I'd been unemployed for two years before being offered the receptionist job. During that time, despite sending out dozens of résumés, the closest I came to employment was as a boxboy at a discount liquor store in my neighborhood. They were offering five bucks an hour, and with the state I was in, I was thrilled by the prospect.

I even blew that one, though, by writing a column about the store before I was ever officially offered the job. In the story, I described what a sleazy, low-rent establishment it was, and I detailed all the personal and psychological problems of the owner (which I had come to learn during my near-daily visits there).

I had assumed he would never see the story, but I was mistaken. One thing I've learned over the years: if you write something about someone, regardless of what publication you're writing for and whether or not you name them, they're going to see it.

This time around, I decided to avoid little mistakes like that. Instead, I called around to a number of people, all of whom had, at one time or another, claimed they owed me favors, in the hope of getting a cushier job lined up before officially giving notice at the *Press*. That's when I discovered how much owed favors meant in a town like New York.

Finding no offers flooding my way by that means, I sat down with my editor, Mr. Strausbaugh, and explained the situation. I was going mad up there, I told him. I was hallucinating, the radio was beginning to talk to me, and I was no longer in a mood to deal with the angry and insane every hour of every day. What's more, I reminded him that I had worked that position longer than anyone in *Press* history, and thought it was about time for a change. I suggested that they might perhaps consider giving me a staff writer job. I'd been writing for the paper every week for over five years—they should know by now that they could count on me.

Much to my surprise, they bought it. Three months after that, they found someone who was willing to take the receptionist job, and I moved back to a desk in an office that I would share with two other staff writers, together with a rotating team of interns, proofreaders, and fact checkers. The new office even had a few windows.

Once having made the move, moments after settling in at the new desk, I froze. I was absolutely terrified of what lay ahead of me. It was the old curse come to life: I'd been given exactly what I wanted, but now had no idea what to do with it. Instead of filling out FedEx slips, taking care of the mail, and dealing with abusive phone calls, I'd be required to do nothing but write, and write a lot. Much more, even, than I'd been writing up until that point. I sat in front of the computer for those first three days petrified, unable to type a single word. My head felt dry and empty. Despite my big talk when meeting with Mr. Strausbaugh, I had no idea what to do. I made lots of trips to the bathroom. I panicked.

Morgan, however, calmed me down the way she did whenever she saw me getting like that, and convinced me it really was a good thing. And though it took a few more days to get the rhythm back, I eventually got down to work, writing not only my column, but weekly human-interest stories, as well as anything else the paper might need to fill space in any given week—book and record reviews, editorials, investigative pieces, previews for upcoming events, anything.

Maybe, I thought at the end of the first week, *it was going to be okay after all.*

chapter eight

A fter spending every night at the same bar for a while, Morgan and I would decide it was time to move on, to find ourselves a new bar to call home. Sometimes it would only take a few weeks at a place to come to this decision; sometimes a few years. It all depended on the bar.

We could simply get bored, or the feel and attitude of a place would change, or it would become too popular. We didn't care much for the popular taverns.

Ray's, the new bar we'd settled in, was all right. Not fancy by any stretch, but quiet and pleasant, with a swell beer selection. We knew the bartenders and they were good to us, and for the most part we were left alone.

Like the others we'd come to rest in over the years, Ray's was in the East Village—a neighborhood which, in mythology, was the down-and-dirty home to cutting-edge artists, musicians, and writers. A mecca for coffeehouse poets and folk singers—and at the same time a dangerous and shadowy world full of junkies and lowlifes and two-bit criminals.

In reality, while all that might have been true a quarter-century ago, the

East Village we were in was overrun with college students and hipsters and tourists, and had become one of the most expensive neighborhoods in the city. The fifth-generation punk-rock kids who hung out panhandling on St. Mark's Place were more often than not wearing shades that cost more than my entire wardrobe.

But it was convenient—Morgan had been living there for a decade—and it was easy to get to, both from the office and from Brooklyn. It was also still easy to find any number of decent as-yet-unsullied taverns there.

One of the things that attracted us to Ray's was the fact that it remained almost completely deserted most weekday afternoons. One advantage of the staff-writing gig was that I could pick up and leave the office whenever I wanted. As the receptionist, I was locked at my desk from eight until six. Now I could leave at one in the afternoon if I liked, which I often did, depending on Morgan's schedule. I'd leave the office, meet up with her, and the two of us would head to the bar.

It was early one August evening. We'd been at Ray's for several hours, had a few in us (much as we did every night), and now were thinking about heading out. The sun was sinking but still bright, and the air was too warm and thick for my taste.

Most afternoons, we'd get our drinks and retire to a back table, near a window that looked out on a walled beer garden. It was the beer garden that first caught our eye—there weren't many of them in New York. When the weather was nice (and sometimes even when it wasn't), we'd go sit out there, where the air was fresher and I could still see a little bit. That day, though, we decided we'd take the air-conditioning instead. The window allowed for a weak breeze and a few scraps of light, which was good.

At about five that afternoon an office party invaded our normally quiet tavern. We'd staked our claim at the back table, but the rest of the bar was far too crowded with youngsters wearing suits and short haircuts, sipping at their martinis, talking about their uninteresting jobs very loudly. Perhaps that's an unfair generalization for me to make about an entire class of people, but having been confronted with people like this so many times in New York—the young, prematurely wealthy, and self-satisfied—I've found that, almost without fail, it holds true. There's a loud arrogance about them, a feigned sophistication that I hate.

It was a bad scene in general, and an unusual one for Ray's. We never had to raise our voices to hear each other while we were there, never had to struggle through a crowd in order to get another round, and the music was always kept at tolerable levels. Scenes like this had led us to abandon other bars in the past. No time for such shenanigans. But tonight we already had our drinks and our table, so we decided to ride it out, cemented in place for at least a few more hours, until we were damned good and ready to leave, praying this was an anomaly and not the way Ray's was headed.

When the time came, we wove our way through the crowd toward the front door. I walked closely behind Morgan, my hands on her hips, my head down, as she led the way, telling me when things were getting narrow, when to watch out for barstools, when things were opening up again. She was very good to me.

Halfway to the door, one of the suit-wearing youngsters reached out with his martini-free hand, plucked my hat off, then dropped it back down on my head. It was a tiny incident, it only took a second, it was completely insignificant. Maybe the beer sloshing around my brain didn't help matters. I should've just let it go, but something in my head exploded, and the rage jumped on me. As we broke through the crowd and headed toward the door, I slipped the folded red-tipped cane out of my bag and gripped it like a club, muttering, mostly to myself, "*Some fuckers deserve a cane against the skull.*"

"What?" Morgan asked, still trying to get us out the door.

"Oh, some asshole just grabbed my hat." The anger was already beginning to ebb away. These things had come to last only a second or two.

"What?" She spun around.

I told her again, not much caring about the incident anymore.

She looked over my shoulder and glared at the group we'd just passed through. They were a hateful lot.

"It's not worth it," I said, touching her arm, regretting having said anything, wanting to avoid any confrontation. "C'mon. I couldn't even tell you who did it." Somehow, simply by scanning the group of them, however, she knew.

She headed back toward the kid in question, as I blindly trailed several feet behind. By the time I got there, I could hear her tearing into him.

"Why would you do that? Why would you do something like that? He *can't see.*"

"Hey, did I know he couldn't see?" the kid asked, his voice prep-school dull, his intonation almost Californian.

"Hey," he continued, spying me behind her. "What's your name?'

"Uhhh . . . Jim," I quietly answered. I was suddenly very tired.

"I'm *Mike*," he barked, as he grabbed my hand firmly and began shaking it. "It's good, right? No harm done?"

Morgan started to say something else, but he cut her off. "Never mind that," he snapped at her, then turned back to me. "It's good, right?" he was still holding onto my hand.

"Just don't touch me again," I said, weakly.

There was a time when Grinch and I—together and independently—would pick fights with people for no reason whatsoever, just to see what they would do. Ironic, perhaps, given how much I'd been bullied when I was growing up.

We targeted political activists of any stripe, Moonies, performance artists, frat boys, punks, anyone. In the end, the only one who ever fought back was a Moonie.

He was chosen at random one afternoon, while he was trying to get University of Wisconsin students to sign a petition "against communism." We didn't care if he was a communist, a Nazi, an acrobat, or a stalwart member of the community—we just hated Moonies, and he was available. For the next forty-five minutes, we followed him up and down streets, alleys, wherever he went with his clipboard, hissing threats at his back.

"Hey," Grinch said. "Ya ever see how much a Moonie *bleeds* when you stick 'em with a knife?" It was a rhetorical question, as neither one of us was carrying a knife at the time.

Finally, in the middle of a narrow and empty side street, the Moonie stopped trying to get away from us. He froze dead in his tracks, threw his clipboard to the ground, spun on his heel, and came running straight toward us, his arms flailing with wacky kung-fu posturings. I actually admired him for that. It took us a while to force him into kung-fu mode, but he finally fought back.

No one else ever did, which we found pretty disappointing.

Now I had become every one of those people we picked on who never fought back. It was like being back in grade school again. I had become a coward, a whiner, impotent and useless. Worse still, I hadn't even stood up for Morgan when she was trying to defend me.

We turned to leave after my hand was freed, the weasel's victorious laughter, and the laughter of his cronies, following us out the door and onto the sidewalk. I felt more than a little sick inside, but I just wanted to get away. *He was a vapor, he wasn't worth it,* I kept telling myself, in a miserable attempt at justification. *I like this bar too much to start a fight here.* In my heart, though, I knew I had failed, I had run away. Fifteen, ten, even five years ago,

I never would've run away, never would've let him step on me or insult my girlfriend that way.

I had failed her, and we both knew it. It wasn't the first time. She deserved so much more than to be treated that way. Now, once again, I felt like a worse weasel than the one we'd just left behind.

Almost fifteen years after our paths diverged, Grinch and I still talked on the phone every few months. He'd tell me about his kids and his job. I'd tell him about the stories I was or wasn't working on, or my most recent physical maladies. His voice still had an anxious shiver to it, as if his body had simply started synthesizing crystal methamphetamine all by its lonesome.

We both had come a long way from our days in Madison. I had survived psych wards and hospitals. Drank. Slid into and out of poverty. Drank more. Wrote stories about the things I had done and the things I was doing. Started having seizures. Was married and divorced. Lost my eyesight. Wrote more stories about that. Answered phones. Fell in love with Morgan. Got a couple of book deals. And now I suddenly found myself terrified that I'd gone soft.

Grinch went through changes, too. After moving around some, he had returned to Chicago, his hometown, and married a woman with a bawdy sense of humor, who also happened to be a corporate bigwig. They had two children, and he got himself a high-paying job in the wine industry. They bought a big condo, got a dog and a couple of cars, and settled down quite nicely.

One night a few weeks after the scene at the bar (which I never mentioned to him), we were on the phone again. We traded old stories, as usual, and everything was fine—but then he started telling me about how much fun he'd been having lately in a managerial position, abusing his minimum-wage employees. Hearing that, I let my own recent frustrations leak out.

"Shit, Grinch," I scolded. "You've become everything we tried to destroy back in Madison." I was sounding a bit too much like a Madison hippie myself, still talking about how much better everything had been in the Sixties. "You've turned into *Dim,* for chrissakes."

"Yeah?" he shot back, without missing a beat, "Well at least I'm not a thirty-four-year-old divorced *alcoholic.*"

I laughed despite the sting. I knew it was a reference to an old punk song, but I also knew that it was true.

By the time I got off the phone with him that night, I was in a foul drunk. I could hardly stand. My sinuses were throbbing from all the smoke I'd sucked up. As usual, I had to be up at five the next morning for work, but sleeping was the last thing I cared about right then.

I reached over the kitchen sink for the whiskey bottle. Poured myself a shot. Then another.

Before crawling, defeated, into bed, I put on an old Killdozer album. I wasn't exactly sure why. It was too late for the punk rock, and it would probably wake the neighbors, but I needed to hear them. Halfway into the album, the lead singer was growling through another loud, grinding, slow tale of woe, betrayal, and failure. When the refrain rolled around, it struck hard for the first time, after I'd heard the song a hundred times before: "*I've decided I've had just about enough of all this, / 'cause I'm just sick and tired of living my life like I don't exist.*"

I did finally get to bed that night, after replaying the song three or four times, but I felt no better for it.

The next morning on my way into work, I passed what appeared to be a pile of discarded clothes crammed into the doorway of a church on Twenty-third Street. I gave it a quick glance, thought nothing more of it, and continued on my way. There was nothing too uncommon about seeing something like that along that stretch of Twenty-third—the church had a soup kitchen, and there was a Salvation Army up the street. People were always leaving bags of clothes on the sidewalk.

Then this particular pile of clothes yelled after me.

"Hey, young man! Meglebarglim!"

I stopped and turned back, trying to decipher what I'd just heard—and confirm that I'd heard anything at all.

"What?" I asked. Then I saw the tiny, pinched old face peering out of the top of the pile.

"I *said,* 'Say, young man, beg your pardon—could you spare an old woman a cigarette?'"

She seemed so polite about it that I couldn't refuse. As I pulled a smoke from the pack and handed it to her, she looked up hard into my face.

"Oh," she said. "I see you're cryin', too."

I reached a finger up and brushed my cheek. She was right. I hadn't even noticed.

chapter nine

S ometimes I missed the chaos of the wild, fuzzy years—the out-of-control drunkenness, the adventure, the pointless destruction, the fights, the broken glass, and the white noise. I chose not to remember how bad those days really were: all the times I puked on myself on the subway, the hopeless and pitiful scrounging for rent money and food, the night I set the apartment on fire (*after* throwing up on myself on the train), the endless stream of humiliations and pain that came with it.

In order for something to happen, I knew I had to get up, go outside, go someplace, do something. I had to make it happen. Then I would remember how the eyes were, and how they—at least in my mind—were preventing me from doing any of that. It's hard to run wild in the streets when you know in the back of your mind that you're going to hit a wall or a garbage can or a parked car at any minute.

When confronted with some serious medical condition—going blind, for instance—there is a dramatic shift in the things foremost in your mind. For some reason, bringing Western Civilization to its knees doesn't seem quite as important as getting to the store and back without injury.

It not only prevented me from reliving the nihilistic days of my youth—it also prevented me from being a very good journalist. At least the kind of journalist I wanted to be, namely Carl Kolchak.

I wanted to be all sorts of things when I was young. An ichthyologist, a seismologist, a theoretical physicist. In each case, these particular career goals were determined by a specific movie. (The movies provided me with most of the answers I needed in life.) The part of me that wanted to be a journalist came as a result of my obsession with a short-lived (1974–75) television series called *Kolchak: The Night Stalker.*

Carl Kolchak (as portrayed by the great Darren McGavin) was a rumpled, frustrated hack reporter working for a second-rate Chicago newspaper who, every week, would come across evidence that the city was being besieged by monsters—vampires, headless bikers, lizard-men, zombies.

He spent every episode battling his frustrated editor (the equally great Simon Oakland) as he tried to gather the evidence he needed, get the story out, and vanquish the monsters at the same time.

It was really something.

Owing to the situation with the eyes, my prospects for monster-chasing around Manhattan were fairly limited. I have trouble seeing buses, let alone vampires. As a result, there were no fisticuffs with the latest reincarnation of Jack the Ripper, and no chasing lizard-men through the sewers, and all the

Hell's Angels I saw over at their clubhouse on Third Street had heads. The stories I did were a bit tamer than that, and mostly conducted via the telephone.

On my way to work one morning, I was trying to figure out the best way to approach that week's subject—an interview with the recent winner of New York City's "Ratcatcher of the Year" award, which was handed out every July to the city's best exterminator.

As I was about to go through the turnstiles in the subway station, a high school girl passed me on her way out.

"You're *ugly*," she hissed. "And you can tell your *momma* I says so."

"Yes, yes, yes," I replied wearily. It was too early to worry about it. I knew I was no prize, and encounters like this no longer surprised me, but still, *Christ.* I hoped it wasn't a portent for the rest of the day.

At ten that morning, against my better judgment, I checked my tape recorder, lit a cigarette, picked up the phone, and dialed the number I'd been given for the Ratcatcher of the Year. When he answered and I confirmed it was him, I set the tape rolling. After some basic questions, I asked if he could tell me about a few of his more intriguing jobs. He seemed ready to tell some stories.

"There was one case where the people in an office were complaining about being bitten," the new champ reminisced. Most exterminators you encounter don't seem too enthusiastic about their work, but this guy was. He was also much better spoken than most. "We installed some monitors, and we caught a bedbug. Now, it was real strange to find a bedbug in an office environment, see? Especially one that was so clean."

"I can imagine."

"As it turned out, when we went in to do a more thorough investigation, the manager told us that he had suspected a particular employee of bringing it in. I asked him to show me that employee's cubicle. And sure enough, you could see in the crevices that there were several stages of these bedbugs. In fact, he had a wooden hanger that he used to put his jacket on. In the split seam, you could actually see them sitting in there. So we were able to definitively determine that this was the point of origin."

My skin began to itch as he told the story, but I didn't let on. I'd had some serious bug issues in my apartment in the past, but now that I could no longer see them, they didn't bother me. Hearing about them, however, was something else.

"Our first approach was to vacuum out as many insects as possible. We subsequently made an application to try to flush out any others that might've been in there. But the key issue was that the manager, being equipped with our report stating that this particular cubicle was the point of origin, was able to address the man, and the man had to admit that he was, indeed, having a problem with bedbugs in his house."

Yes, well.

"At this point," the Ratcatcher went on, "they asked one of our entomologists to take a look and see what the extent was. Our senior entomologist had gone there, and said that there were probably several *thousand* bugs in this very small apartment. Every crack and crevice in the entire apartment, every piece of furniture had bedbugs in it. He opened up the closet where the gentleman kept his suits, and lifted the lapel of every jacket, and under every lapel there were fifty to a hundred bedbugs."

I gave up on subtlety and began scratching myself openly as I sat at my desk. My ankles, my hands, the back of my head. "I can see how something like that might wreck your whole day," I offered.

"Yeah, well, the question comes to mind, how can you have so many parasites in an apartment and not have somebody complain about being bit at night, right? Then we find out that he has a severe drinking problem, and he would get so drunk he would pass out and not feel anything."

Yeah, I guess I've been there, I thought.

"It would've been quite expensive to try and eradicate that level of population," he went on. "I think that right after that, they let the gentleman go. That was the easiest way; otherwise, he would've continued to bring these things in and continue to subject other people to these parasites. . . . That was a strange situation, something that doesn't happen often."

"I would hope not, yeah."

He went on to tell stories about armies of roaches and wood ants, and his struggles to outsmart some of the world's cleverest rats.

"For all the years I've been doing it now, I've found that you can run into a situation almost monthly that you've never seen before. It's constantly intriguing."

"I think I'm starting to see that myself," I replied.

I needed to take a walk after I hung up the phone. A drink might help, too. His stories, however gleefully he'd told them, affected me in a very profound and disturbing way. Sort of like that rabbit story my folks had told me.

It was more than the Ratcatcher's tales, though, that left me feeling antsy and off-kilter. Lots of things had been gathering. The scene at Ray's, the stab from Grinch—even the volume of the noise in the office and that nasty little hussy in the subway. So many other insignificant and petty frustrations. I'd tried to shove them all to the back of my consciousness, but their sheer collective bulk was starting to eat at me, making it hard to concentrate on anything. I was pissed at myself and pissed at the world. Sometimes it's the stupidest of things that can push me hardest in that direction.

I took the elevator from the fourteenth floor and hit the streets, still irritated and itchy, still limping off the growth on my heel. I turned south, head down, eyes unfocused, stomach turning clockwise as I argued silently (I think) with people and machines. I tried to stay on Seventh Avenue because Seventh was wide and uncluttered, more easily navigated without the cane, so long as the sun was out. I was in no mood for the cane. When I hit Twenty-third Street, I turned left. Twenty-third was wide and uncluttered as well.

There were plenty of people around, but they were spread out widely enough that I could dodge the fuzzy shapes.

I continued walking past my usual subway stop, turned south again at Sixth Avenue, and kept walking. All I knew was that I just had to keep walking. That usually helped. The sidewalks along Sixth Avenue narrowed considerably, but people stayed in their lanes for the most part, and things kept moving.

I could feel both the itching and the frustration evaporating with each block I passed, just like I hoped it would, until I hit Nineteenth Street.

It was there that I found myself reduced to a crawl by the slow-moving guy in front of me. I wasn't as annoyed by this as I usually might be, though— he had every excuse to be moving slowly. Dragging the left foot, limping heavily, head lolling to one side, both arms curled up in front of him like a squirrel.

Oh, man.

Then, after just a few steps—Christ, I saw this coming—he got his left foot caught in a plastic shopping bag. He never broke stride. He continued plodding along, each dragged step cementing that bag around his foot more securely—*shhk-klomp, shhk-klomp, shhk-klomp.*

Part of me was fascinated by the slapstick potential here (would he hit the coiled garden hose next? Or the bucket?), while part of me wanted to help him get that thing off his foot. But what do you do? If I just tried to step on the bag from behind in the hope that he would simply and easily step out of it, there was a good chance I'd send him sprawling to the pavement, probably breaking both of his arms in the process.

So do I tap him on the shoulder instead? Do I ask him to stop? What? Jesus, what do I do?

All the while, he's forging onward, *shhk-klomp,* either unaware of the bag, or utterly humiliated, knowing there wasn't a goddamn thing he could do about it.

In the end, I did what most people would do—I turned yellow, pulled my eyes away from the bag, and tried to pass him when I got the chance.

This was difficult, given the oncoming foot traffic and my own lack of coordination and depth perception. Still, I gave it a shot. Everything was going fine until I came alongside him. Only then did I notice that, with his curled and crippled left hand, he was manipulating a red-and-white cane, just like the one I had folded up in my bag.

Aww, Christ, he's blind, too? Will it never end?

The yellow streak on my back suddenly grew wider and deeper, and I shot ahead, listening as the *shhk-klomp* slowly receded behind me, finally swallowed up by the noise of the traffic and the other pedestrians.

At Sixteenth Street, I hit a red light.

As I stood there waiting, praying the light would change soon so I could get the hell out of there to a place where I could forget about my cowardice, I heard it again. It was getting louder—and closer.

Shhk-klomp, shhk-klomp . . .

Aww, man.

The light didn't change. In a moment, the sound was directly behind me. There it stopped.

Then I heard a wet, strangled voice ask, "*Sssomebonny hep me?*"

The crowd around us on the corner, as should have been expected, vanished in several different directions at once, leaving the two of us alone.

I was feeling that newly discovered sense of "remorse" as it was, so I stepped around next to him and held out an elbow.

"Here's my arm," I told him. Once he had a firm hold, I looked down at the bag, put my foot on one edge of it, and said, "Lift your left foot."

As he lifted the foot, the bag stayed tangled around his ankle, and he began to stumble backward.

Then he began to scream.

"*Aaannnhh! Whan's hammenineen?!*"

Oh, Christ.

"*Ahhhhnnnhh!*"

Fortunately, with all the flailing about he'd been doing, he had broken free of the bag. I helped him, as much as I could, to regain his balance.

"It was just a plastic bag," I told him. "It's gone now."

He began to calm down, and the light changed. "There's the light," I said, "Here we go."

We stepped out into the street. About halfway across, he said quietly, "Hang you fo' hehlmee' me."

"That's okay. You gonna be all right once we get across here?"

He made a small noise that I took to be a confirmation.

On the opposite corner, I stopped. He let go of my arm, and got the cane ready again.

"Well, be careful," I said, waving uselessly. At the same time, I was thinking, *Yeah, I don't have much of anything to complain about.*

Lord knows through the years, and all the things I'd done, I'd incurred some hefty karmic debts that would need to be repaid one of these days. Not that I believe in karma, not really, but it's still worth considering now and again. And while that little scene certainly wasn't wiping any slates clean, it might've helped polish a little smudge somewhere. Probably just enough to balance out passing him in the first place without stopping to help him with that bag.

Nevertheless, it was something.

I decided to postpone that drink until later. I turned back toward the office and lit a smoke. There was a deli a block away from work. I stopped in there and picked up a ham sandwich and a soda, then returned to my desk.

I had opened the soda, swallowed my afternoon pills, and started eating as I scanned the news wires for anything interesting when the phone rang.

"Hey, doctor," a voice said. It was my editor, Mr. Strausbaugh, whose office was two doors down the hall.

"Hey," I replied. "What goes on?"

"Well, you know that Squiggy interview you turned in?"

"Of course I know it. I wrote it." Two weeks earlier, I'd interviewed David Lander, the guy who played Squiggy on *Laverne and Shirley*. I was expecting the interview to be run as a feature.

"Well, we aren't gonna be able to use it."

I could feel my mood beginning to turn again.

"And why the hell not? It was a great interview—the guy's been hiding the fact that he has MS for over a decade, and now he's coming out about it. It's a great story. And what's more, he bad-mouths Richard Fleischer and tells funny stories about *On the Air*—"

"Doctor, it's not running."

"Why?" I still demanded to know.

"Why? Because nobody cares what Squiggy has to say."

It was a refrain I was hearing more and more often, with "Squiggy" being replaced with any number of names, from Ned Beatty to "the guy who directed *Slaves of the Cannibal God*." I should've been getting used to it, but I wasn't.

"But—" I pleaded desperately, "it's *Squiggy*!"

The afternoon didn't get much better after that. I tried transcribing the interview with the Ratcatcher, but hearing all those stories repeated was making me itch again. What's more, the youngsters in the office with me were getting loud and rambunctious again. They always did in the afternoon, playing grab-ass and holding freshman-year philosophical debates. Even if I'd wanted to finish transcribing the interview, the increasing noise levels would've made it impossible. Instead, I turned back to the news wires, scanning for any new and interesting tales of human depravity.

By the end of the day, my body was numb, all except for the left leg, which, because of that thing on my heel, threatened to buckle under me every time I put any weight on it. With regrets, I called Morgan and told her that I thought I was going to have to skip getting together at the bar that night and head straight back to Brooklyn instead.

At a little before five, I limped out of the office, then limped down the street, then limped onto a train. At least I didn't have to drag a heavy gray mailbag along with me the way I used to.

Much to my amazement, I found a seat on the train, slid the magnifying glass out of my bag, along with the large-print (though not nearly large enough) edition of Samuel Beckett's first novel. It had to be Beckett after a day like that. Even with the large print and the magnifying glass, as I bent low over the page the only fragment I was able to decipher was, ". . . the sleep of pure terror. Compare the opossum." That struck me as unduly profound at the time, and I made a note to remember it. I gave up trying to read any further in order to figure out just what the hell Mr. Beckett might've meant by that, and put everything away. That done, I sat back and waited, my eyes as dim and sore and worthless as the rest of me.

I don't know what stop it was when they came aboard. One of the bad ones, I'd guess. It doesn't really matter. The moment I heard something, some voices, from the other end of the train, I knew that I was in for it.

It wasn't the ghostly mariachi band this time, no, even though that's whom I would've expected. It was their replacement act in the realm of cheap symbolism.

Instead of being blessed by the appearance of a Greek chorus in the form of a mariachi band, I was cursed with one in the form of a doo-wop gospel quartet. That's the last group of people you want to see when all you want to do is weep from exhaustion and frustration. Making things worse was the fact that, unlike the mariachi band, I could understand what they were saying.

"Oh, Jesus Christ," I muttered aloud, as they headed down the aisle toward me, their voices bright and lively and full of some friendly religious fervor. Everyone around me seemed happy to see them—the other passengers were smiling broadly and nodding their heads in time with the music while digging into their pockets and purses for change.

The quartet broke into their rendition of "This Little Light of Mine." Ever since I was a kid in Sunday School, I've hated that song. It saddened me, and left me filled with visions of fire. This time around, the quartet helped me hate it even more by changing the lyrics.

God's the one who got you up this morning! they sang cheerfully, as if this were a good thing, *I'm gonna let it shine!*

"Well," I muttered aloud again, not caring who heard me, or what they might have to say about it. "At least now I know where to lay the blame for everything."

They marched past me to the other end of the train, smiling, singing, collecting more change than I've ever seen any train performer collect in a single pass, while my weariness deepened and my mood slipped from dirty yellow to flat black.

When the train reached my stop, I hobbled off, dragged myself up the stairs, lit a smoke, and limped slowly homeward.

I was stewing through a tired and quiet rage as I strolled painfully down the street, looking forward to eating and going to bed, praying I'd finally be able to sleep. Then I passed an enormous cardboard refrigerator box. It was sitting all alone in the middle of the sidewalk, like the monolith in *2001*. I didn't know why it was there—though I hazarded a guess that someone who lived in one of the nearby buildings had recently purchased a new refrigerator.

I stopped a moment, and squinted at it. It was dredging something up, I could feel it. Didn't know what it was yet, though. *Should I find myself a thigh bone?* I thought. *Is that it?* Memory is such an odd beast.

I stepped around the box, which was a good six inches taller than I was, and continued on my way.

With each step, I knew I was getting closer to what that box was stirring in me. I used to play with boxes as a kid, but that wasn't it. Pretended they were tanks or submarines or battleships in the dark, phantom-infested, cement-floored basement of the little duplex in Green Bay.

This was different. A classroom was involved. And a tapping sound. And a lot of small voices, laughing. And darkness, and fear.

By the time I turned the corner, I had it.

Third grade. Webster Elementary. Mrs. Hackmuller's class. *Hackmuller.* What a fucking awful name. But fitting.

She decided one day, for reasons far beyond me, that it was the duty of the students in her class to put on a little fair for the first-graders of the school. Teachers always seem to think that things like that are a good idea.

There would be games and snacks and entertainment. Everyone would leave feeling buoyant and satisfied, happy to be alive at such a magical time.

As duties were assigned, some of my classmates were told that they'd be running games or concession stands. And I was told that I would be . . . a clown.

More than just a stupid, mincing clown (the kind that so terrified me)— I was to be a jack-in-the-box clown. I had no idea what she was talking about. She was insane.

Here was her idea. She had this clown suit. She also had a refrigerator box. Put the clown suit on the kid, put the kid in the refrigerator box, have the kid jump out of the refrigerator box and voilà—instant, foolproof entertainment.

She chose three of us. Mike Ruppert (who would be shotgunned to death by his brother at the age of eighteen), Greg Alpman (a big dumb kid), and me (the scrawny one who couldn't believe that he was about to be humiliated this way).

The classroom was decorated with gaily colored streamers and pictures and balloons. Desks were moved out of the way, tables were set up, and games were readied.

The fair was scheduled to run from three, when school let out, until five-thirty. Each "Clown-in-the-Box" would be expected to perform for forty-five minutes. Jump out of the box. Get back in the box. Jump out of the box. Get back in the box. And so forth.

Mike would be first, then Greg, then me. I was glad of that. After an hour and a half, I figured the shtick would've pretty much played itself out, and no one would be paying attention anymore.

What I found particularly sad back then was the fact that the refrigerator box in question wasn't disguised at all. It was just a damned brown cardboard box with AMANA or KENMORE or FRIGIDAIRE printed on the side, together with the product specifications. A red Magic Marker had been taken to it some, but to no great effect.

As the fair progressed, I wandered the classroom, amongst the happy children and patient adults, occasionally swinging by to watch Mike and Greg's technique. They seemed to be enjoying themselves. They'd pop out of the top of the box, much to the delight of the children sitting on the floor around them, make faces, talk in funny voices, what have you. Once in a while, Mrs. Hackmuller would come by and ask loud questions through the side of the box, while Mike or Greg were crouched in the darkness, awaiting the perfect moment to suddenly appear again, surprising everyone.

Then it was my turn. Greg slipped out of the one-piece clown outfit (which by now was soaked in the sweat of two people) and handed it to me, and I stepped into it.

It hung off my body like a damp shower curtain, revealing more than it covered. Greg tipped the box on its side, and I crawled into it. Then he set it upright again.

None of this had ever been rehearsed in any way. The box I ran into on the sidewalk was half a foot taller than I am now. When I was eight, a box of the same size would've been almost twice my height (I was a very short child). So while Mike and Greg—both of them being on the tall side—could very easily pop out of the top, as is expected of a Clown-in-the-Box, I found that the best I could manage was to punch a hand through the top and wave.

That seemed foolish unless you were putting on a puppet show, so I did the next-best thing, which, in my mind, was the first-best thing all along.

I sat in the darkness, knees to my chest, at the bottom of that box, un-moving, unentertaining, for forty-five minutes, until it was time to go home. Mrs. Hackmuller knocked on the side of the box after the first ten minutes of silence, called to me, told me to come out and say hi to the kids—even opened up the top and peeked in once, whispering a mild threat—but I wouldn't budge. No sir. Just sat there.

Thinking back on the day, I could understand it perfectly, that quest for isolation. I'd been doing it since I was very young, and I'd been doing much more of it lately.

In spite of everything, in spite of the fact that things were going better than they ever had before and that I was more relaxed and comfortable (regardless of how that particular day had gone), I also found that I was growing increasingly less interested in talking to people. My stomach tightened up whenever I ran into someone I knew on the street or in a bar. There were a few exceptions, of course, like Morgan and my folks, but in general, I just didn't want to see anyone anymore. Even telephone calls, I'd found, exhausted me, and after five or ten minutes, my mind would start to wander and I'd wish I could just hang up. The immobilizing shyness of my early youth seemed to be returning.

As a result of the books, and the fact that my picture had appeared here and there, more people were stopping me on the sidewalks and in the subways and at the bars. Most of them were extraordinarily neighborly and cordial folks who just wanted to say a few words and then move on. Still, they made me very nervous. It wasn't their fault. Not at all, and in a way, sure, of course I was happy to hear that people enjoyed whatever it was that I was doing. I didn't want to appear rude and didn't want to be an asshole when this sort of thing happened, but I'm afraid it might have seemed that way at times, because all I wanted to do was hide.

It wasn't just the strangers on the street, either. It was old friends and old co-workers—people I respected and with whom I'd spent many happy hours. I was frightened of something I couldn't put my finger on. In general I was relaxed and happy, yes—but I was also terrified. People still fascinated me—the things they did and the things they said—but I preferred to observe these things from a distance. I guess that's one of the many contradictions we all carry around with us.

When I finally reached my apartment that night, I wasn't feeling much better. I opened the first of that evening's several beers. Several, maybe, but not nearly enough.

At four the next morning, my big, happy retarded cat started banging his head against the window again, while the small, evil one poked one of her tiny white paws into my open and snoring mouth, extended her claws, and sliced the length of my tongue open neat as can be. I knew then that I was in it for a while. I should've just kept my damn-fool mouth shut when that doo-wop group sang their stupid little song.

A long with the newly sliced tongue, it seemed that nearly my entire body was becoming overrun with foreign growths of one kind or another. Within a year after I'd had an eyeball-sized cyst profession- ally removed from my left ankle, it had grown back almost as big as it was be- fore. The smaller, pea-sized lump on my left heel still had me limping. Then another lump appeared beneath my left ear. It might've been the lymph node—it was in the right area—but I chose instead to believe that it was nothing more than an ingrown hair. That one seemed to be getting smaller after a couple of weeks. Or at least narrower.

Then something appeared on the left side of the bridge of my nose. An- other oozing cyst of some sort, though not so big as an eyeball. Still another one began appearing and disappearing with some regularity on the tailbone.

My watch kept stopping, too.

After taking a quick inventory, I realized that all of the cysts and pustules were erupting exclusively on the left side of my body. The right side remained smooth and relatively unblemished. It was pasty, but at least not lumpy, grotesque, and overrun with horrible growths and lesions.

Even the dying watch was wrapped around my left wrist.

Then my ophthalmologist told me that a cataract was slowly developing over my right eye, clouding what little was left of the vision there. The right eye had always been the stronger of the two, which made this news especially distressing. What made it funny was the fact that it was completely unrelated (medically, anyway) to anything else that was wrong with that eye.

I don't bring up these things merely as an update of my continued physical degeneration or to bemoan my lot. No, something else was going on.

Morgan was the first to suggest a right brain/left brain explanation. She hinted that maybe it was the result of an unconscious struggle between the two hemispheres of the brain, between the logical left half, which mostly controls the right side of the body, and the creative right half that controls the left. Or vice versa. I could never keep them straight.

Even though she was joking when she brought it up, I was more than willing to accept her theory. It made sense. My brain had been feeling dry, used up, and empty. Spent. Worn to the weft and filled with rue. Numb.

Maybe my growths were an expression of the frustration or desperation on the part of my right brain, not unlike what goes on in David Cronenberg's *The Brood,* in which Samantha Eggar's rage is first expressed as a collection of ugly eruptions on the surface of the flesh, and later as a pack of murderous dwarves.

It wasn't just the creative right side turning the left half of my body into some sort of modernist sculpture. The logical hemisphere had been failing me as well. Shutting down when I most needed it, or prompting the worst conceivable things to come out of my mouth at the worst possible times.

It felt like my brain was intentionally fucking me up.

The notion—if only in the form of a metaphor—that I was still being pursued by demons, haunted by Bad Spirits, returned. In the past, I'd blamed them for everything from simple accidents to slips of the tongue, pointless attacks by and upon others, and suicide attempts. I knew there had to be something more to it than what feeble-minded doctors had once called a "mixed personality disorder."

Were these spirits and demons, now camped out in the hemispheres of my brain, battling each other for supremacy? Or had they instead joined forces, like in the comic books or on one of the wrestling shows, in order to put me in the ground by whatever means necessary?

Borrowing another metaphor from Freud, I could speculate that my id and superego were beating the crap out of each other, with no ego in be-tween them to referee. It might make sense, if we think of ego as something akin to the "soul." I was, after all, convinced that mine had long since fled. Or if it hadn't exactly "fled," it sure as hell had lost most of its get-up-and-go.

I'd talked and joked for years about my soulless predicament (and thus my susceptibility to demonic assault), but had it finally, actually happened? Had my soul died while I wasn't paying attention?

134

It's a condition in which more than a few of us might find ourselves ensnared, if we stopped to consider it for too long.

We work at soul-crushing jobs, eat lunch at the same place every day, listen to the same radio stations, watch the same television shows, do what we can to make more money, avoid conflict, or ignore the fact that we don't really give a good goddamn about the person we married. We can do all these things without thinking about it, except maybe for some vague notion in the back of our heads that maybe things could be better, somehow.

It's an old story, of course. A very old one. Nothing new there. Some trace it back to the Industrial Revolution, some call it the fundamental condition of modern man, some call it existentialism. Myself, I think it goes back much farther than that. I think it's always been with us. And, as always, if you ignore those feelings of unease and dissatisfaction, eh, they'll pass in time. As those feelings vanish, what's left of our spirit goes with it. Sometimes it takes a solid body-blow to make us start thinking again.

I was living in Philly with my then-wife Laura when the seizures first appeared. After a dozen doctors weren't able to diagnose what was going on, I came to the conclusion that I was (not surprisingly) the subject of demonic possession. I knew in my heart that there weren't really demons afoot in the world—but they made for a handy and delightful explanation. I was no longer surprised that in the Middle Ages epileptics were taken to be possessed. It sure can look like it sometimes—spasms exploding out of nowhere, strange voices spilling from your mouth and saying all the terrible, painfully honest things you can't remember having said later. I had almost all the symptoms, as laid out by the Vatican, of someone who was possessed by a demon.

Laura was a scientist, an extremely rational woman, but she saw what happened when these things hit, and for a while there, I even had her believing that I was possessed.

When I brought this theory of mine up with my doctor at the time—none of the dozen or so specialists she had sent me to had yet mentioned the word "seizures" to me, never even hinted that it might be a logical explanation—she suggested that I consider looking for a shrink, but that before I did, I should go see a neurologist. The neurologist she sent me to was able to take a few pictures, point easily at the brain lesion, then give me a simple explanation, together with a bottle of pills.

I found that disappointing. I sort of had my heart set on the whole demonic-possession thing. So who's to say that the brain lesion wasn't just Satan in another form? Maybe it was Satan's vacation house. Or maybe those Bad Spirits who had been shadowing me for so long had finally chosen to simply take up residence, in order to save on travel expenses. It would have explained a lot, and provided me with a handy-dandy excuse for damn near anything.

A decade after the seizures were diagnosed as being non-demonic in nature, the Vatican admitted that, yes indeed, exorcisms were not only still going on, but the number of exorcists employed by parishes around the globe was increasing dramatically. They also wrote up a new set of ritual guidelines regarding exorcisms—the first since 1614. The only major difference in the new ritual was that exorcists were encouraged to consult physicians and psychiatrists before they went all crazy with the holy water.

That made a hell of a lot of sense. The television tabloid shows of the era often ran bits about cases of demonic possession, and in more instances than not, the footage they showed of the "possessed" person made it clear, to me at least, that they were suffering from the same condition I was, and that a quick MRI would likely reveal as much. Either that, or they were just having a really bad temper tantrum and were in need of a spanking.

Vatican officials remained mum on the actual number of exorcisms taking place every year, claiming they didn't keep records of such things. A year after the new edicts were released, however, it was made public that Pope John Paul II had attempted, and failed, to exorcise a demon from a local seventeen-year-old girl who'd been getting uppity. The story appeared in the *New York Post* under the remarkable headline DEVIL BEATS POPE.

Not long after reading of his failure, my own non-demonic seizures began to creep back up on me with a frequency and a force I hadn't experienced in years. Despite gobbling a thousand milligrams of Tegretol—my anti-convulsive medication—every day, they were once again hitting me at home, on the street, at work. In most cases they arose when I was under some stress, but not always. Sometimes they came out of nowhere. It was becoming a nuisance, and it was beginning to worry me more than a little. I'd even tried to make an appointment with my neurologist in order to see what insight he could offer concerning this latest barrage, only to discover that he was on a fishing vacation in Cambodia for the next several weeks. I was adrift for a while.

This was bad news. I had been making a concerted effort in recent years to be more pleasant, calmer, more decent to the people around me. It all went back to the question of remorse. I knew that the uncontrollable rage of my youth and early adulthood had hurt people I cared about, but at the time I didn't care. The rage was all that mattered. The rage was my energy source. It was a hateful world, I felt, and I was giving back to it in kind, no matter what or who got in the way. I had stomped through life with no regrets whatsoever. Quite the opposite. I did what I wanted, what I thought was funny. I was often cruel and rude and nasty, because those things had become my aesthetic. I saw the general public as a collection of gutless, mindless sheep, thought I was better and smarter then they were (thanks to a grotesque misreading of Nietzsche's concept of the *Übermensch* and the Will to Power), and went about proving it by being an asshole.

Now, though, I was trying to curb that. I didn't regret the vandalism or the thieving, the attempted arson or the large-scale pranks Grinch and I had pulled. Those were, I freely admit, a lot of fun. But I was looking back and feeling bad about hurting all those people along the way who didn't deserve it: my parents, old friends, people who had been trying to be nice to me, Morgan. I was still fucking up, but I was trying.

With the sudden return of the seizures, I was worried that perhaps the

Tegretol I was taking was doing little more than tamping the anger down, keeping it at bay for a while. I was afraid it was still there, still boiling just beneath the surface, and that one of these days it would all come out at once, and the results would be devastating.

One fit began making its gentle presence known while Morgan and I were sitting at the back table in Ray's around five o'clock on a Tuesday evening. It was sweltering outside, and even in the air-conditioning, the sweat wasn't drying.

I felt the beginnings of the familiar slow burn at the base of my skull, like a nudging elbow in the brain. Within a few short minutes, the choking, inescapable stuttering kicked in. Once I hit the stuttering point, there's pretty much no turning back; it's only going to get worse. All I can do is pray that I don't do something awful before it subsides.

I hated putting Morgan through something like this. She'd seen them before, but they never got any easier.

Soon my face was contorting spasmodically and my body was trembling, I was hissing obscenities, and my teeth had latched onto the meat of my right index finger. I didn't notice until later that I had punctured the skin. The best thing I can do when this happens is take myself home. I'm not going to be any good to anybody for a while—and I could possibly pose a danger to them if things really got out of hand. I needed to isolate myself, and fast. In most cases, Morgan would insist on staying with me, on helping out however she could—but in this instance, I knew it was for the best.

I was able to get on a train, which, thankfully, wasn't too crowded. I'd replaced chewing on my hands with chewing on my tongue and lower lip. Nobody chose to sit near me.

Something was going wrong. I'd had seizures before, with all these same symptoms, but they usually passed in twenty minutes or half an hour—and those were the long ones. More often than not, the fits were there and gone in a few seconds. This one showed no signs of going anywhere in the near future. It had its claws in me now, and it was getting stronger.

When I finally got home (after holding myself together as well as I could on the train) and had locked the apartment door behind me, it detonated across my body. I was on the floor, twitching and growling and barking. I couldn't control my arms or legs. Two hours later, while the most violent spasms seemed to have passed, waves of low-level temblors still washed up and down my spine. I forced myself to go to bed, where the chances of seriously injuring my two cats or myself were reduced. Even in bed, however, my eyes glaring maniacally and uselessly around in the darkness, my teeth still slowly gnawing away on what was left of my bleeding tongue, I couldn't sleep. Every time I felt like I was about to drift off, another wave of shakes and spasms and rage would pass through me like an erratic electrical current, and I'd be staring into the darkness again, worn out, beaten, sore, and wide awake.

Finally, about three or four the next morning, my eyes closed. These things will drain everything right the hell out of you. I might've still been shaking, but at least I wouldn't notice anymore.

By the time I awoke again the next morning, things still hadn't completely left me. My face was convulsing as I stood under the hot water in the shower, my hands twitched violently as I tried to shave. I put myself together somehow and, for reasons I can't fully comprehend—apart from that damnable, persistent Protestant work ethic—headed in to work, where I tried to do my job without attacking any co-workers or shrieking.

If I was lucky, my editor, Mr. Strausbaugh, would have a copy of the Vatican's new exorcism ritual lying around his office. You could usually count on him for things like that.

The inside of my head felt like it was aflame, but the major tremors seemed to have died away, leaving only a persistent, low-level hum behind. That was still enough to wrack me up and keep me from thinking straight. The thing about not getting any sleep (this was a bit of a kicker) was that exhaustion always makes a seizure more likely. And here I was, exhausted, still trying to shake one after, Christ, what, seventeen hours? I'd never had one last that long before, and it was still threatening to explode again into something that could drop me to the floor.

I held myself tight to my chair, my fingers shaking too badly to type worth a shit, just trying not to let things loose again. *Why the hell had I come in here?* I wondered.

By four that afternoon, the fire had almost burned itself out. I was numb and drained, but I was no longer shaking or hissing. Twenty-three hours. That was a new record for me. My tongue felt like ground chuck and I could still taste metallic blood, but I didn't feel like slamming my head in the door anymore. I left the office and met up with Morgan, and we went back to the bar where it had all started the day before, sat at the same table even, and had a few peaceful beers. I was beat, but I was glad to be there with her. I wanted to apologize and prove to her that I wasn't going nuts again.

"The demons've been after me bad," I explained, my voice rough, my speech slower than usual.

Thinking back on it, there are better ways to prove that I'm not nuts than to start up with the demon talk. She understood, though—after all, she'd been through twelve years of Catholic school. Plus, I had explained the seizures to her long ago. It didn't make them any more pleasant to be around.

Later that night after getting home, I watched a bit of television as I ate my sandwich and then decided to go to bed early.

I piled my clothes on the chair by my desk and went into the bathroom. I brushed my teeth as I always did, took my pills—whole lotta good they were doing—and prepared to step into the shower.

That's when I noticed that something felt odd. It wasn't pain, exactly, or discomfort of any kind. Something just felt different about my right foot. I looked down toward the floor.

My right foot was covered in blood. It was mostly dried, but the surface was still sticky. It covered the top of my foot, running down the sides, across and between the toes. It was thick and dark.

I think most anyone would find this at least mildly disconcerting. What do you do when you find a part of your body unexpectedly covered in blood? How do you properly react? Strangely, I didn't panic or begin to flail about. I'd had enough of that sort of thing over the past day.

I sat down on the cool edge of the tub and searched over my foot carefully, feeling for a wound, a cut, an open sore of any kind beneath the coating of blood. A distinct, sharp pain anywhere. The foot operation had taken place the previous January and had since completely healed, despite the fact that the cyst had grown back. What's more, the operation had taken place on the left foot, not the right, so that wasn't it. There was nothing I could find. No obvious source at all. I'd been wearing socks until just before I entered the bathroom, and they seemed fine. Since the blood was mostly dried, it hadn't just happened. It was almost as if it had just seeped out of my flesh.

Not being in any pain, finding it all a bit puzzling but not too worrisome, I climbed into the shower and washed the blood away. My foot seemed perfectly fine again. Not a mark. I climbed out of the shower, dried myself, and had a smoke. Shortly thereafter, I went to bed. Then I forgot about it.

It wasn't until I was on the subway the next morning that the word "stigmata" entered my head. Maybe it wasn't a demon at all this time, I realized.

The previous day had been Passover; it was just a day or two until Good Friday. We were getting into that stigmata season, all right.

Pre-fifteenth-century trustworthy statistics about bleeding palms are awfully difficult to come by. Even though there had been twenty stigmatics in the nineteenth century, no pope in recent memory had the stigmata. Nor, so far as I'm aware, had Mother Teresa, Princess Diana, or Elvis. So what the hell good were they? I had a friend once who, after getting stupid drunk at my kitchen table one night, explained that he had it. He proudly displayed the holes in his hands, but upon closer examination, it seemed the holes had recently been scratched open with a nail. While the nails may have made sense, I didn't think it much counted if you did it to yourself.

But did stigmata affect feet? It would seem so, logically, but you never much heard about it. Hands and sides, yes, even the occasional forehead, but feet? I admittedly didn't know too much about such things, so I made a few telephone calls to some lapsed Catholics and discovered that yes, indeed, feet are fair game.

What the hell was happening this time? If it was stigmata, why had it only affected one foot? Why didn't I get the full package deal? And why did it pass so quickly?

I thought on these questions for a long time. They kept me occupied for most of the morning. Everybody thought that I was joking about the blood on my foot, so they didn't take my questions seriously at all. They just laughed and sent me on my way. Still, it ate at me—can a person get a *mild* dose of stigmata?

A few hours later while I was eating lunch, the answer appeared to me, fully formed. It made perfect sense, too. If what I was dealing with was indeed stigmata, then it only affected me peripherally because, obviously enough, I was raised a Lutheran. I didn't have a vaguely Catholic bone in my body. What's more, I was no longer even a believer.

That much solved, now the question remained: Why was I being burdened with an affliction of the most holy among Catholics?

(This is simply how I think about things, sometimes.)

It took a few beers with Morgan that night before the solution to this particular conundrum arrived.

In order to answer the question, I realized, I had to go back to a point before the blood (or rather, Blood) appeared. I had to go back to that peculiarly tenacious seizure, which had ended only a few hours before I noticed what was happening with my right foot.

Accounts I had read of other, more traditional cases of stigmata over the centuries—nuns and priests whose hands, sides, and feet would spew great gouts of blood for years at a stretch—also oftentimes seemed to involve shakings and speaking in tongues and other strange behavioral tics. Holy visions and whatnot. Those tics were put down as visitations—possessions, if you will—by the Holy Spirit.

That was the answer I was looking for. That seizure, during which I trembled and flopped around and spoke in tongues of a sort (at least *chewed* on my tongue) was no doubt a visitation by the Holy Spirit. In my case, instead of entering my body, filling me with the joyous inner light and the peace that passes all understanding, the Holy Ghost tripped up, found Himself inside me, and was fighting to get out, having realized only after the fact that He had made a terrible, horrible mistake. After a day of struggling, He finally discovered his portal of escape through my right foot. Being, as He is, a spiritual creature, that of course would explain the lack of any visible exit wound.

Things pretty much returned to normal that evening, since I'd finally understood clearly what had happened in the previous two days. That night, when I took off my socks before getting into the shower, I looked down at my foot expectantly. It was clean as a whistle. Not a drop of blood anywhere. I was vaguely disappointed. Just as disappointed as I had been back in 1989, when the neurologist showed me the MRI and told me that I wasn't really possessed by a demon.

I like the metaphors. I like the battles between Good and Evil. Hell, with the cats, I'm living with that all the time, my apartment having been transformed into a miniature battlefield, where the war between Good and Evil never ends.

The question in this case was, how could a metaphor draw blood?

I was perhaps too willing, even eager, to dismiss it all as just another story. Just Something Else That Happened. And consciously, that's exactly what I did. But it was becoming clear that certain obsessions had been hanging around me for as long as I could remember. I wasn't sure what to make of that. Jesus in my room, crucifixions, demonic pursuit and attack, and now this.

I didn't actually believe in anything, so why was I so smitten with all this crap? Perhaps I could blame Carl Jung—which helps explain why I've always avoided Jungians with the same fervor with which I've avoided any other spiritual type. Or maybe I was simply looking at my life in horror-movie terms. That would make sense—I **cared** more about movies than I did about religion—which is why I began to think as the days passed that the blood didn't represent evidence of stigmata at all, but rather the birth of a murderous dwarf.

On a Thursday evening a few months after the stigmatum or dwarf appeared and then vanished, Morgan and I found ourselves in midtown Manhattan for some reason. This was strange, since we generally tried to avoid Midtown at all costs. Midtown—what most people who don't live here think of when they think of New York, with its endless skyscrapers butted up against one another, its sidewalks packed with fabulous beautiful people, its streets jammed with taxis—was a nightmare. It was an area of town that contained too little of what we were ever looking for, and too much of what we hated. On any given day, it was overpopulated with oblivious, self-absorbed, uninteresting, cell-phone-packing jackasses; it was too loud, too expensive, and it smelled bad—and it was damned hard to find a decent bar.

That evening, however, traffic both on the streets and on the sidewalks had dissipated. We'd even found a place to drink for a while.

By the time we left, we'd each had a few, and now we were holding each other upright, stumbling toward the lights and traffic of the nearest avenue.

Maybe it was Fifth, maybe Sixth. We weren't really sure. I stopped a moment to light a smoke, finally, and try and figure out where the nearest useful subway station might be.

"We're in the what," I asked, "the Fifties?"

"Yeah—Fifty-third, I think. We'll find out."

"Okay, then, I think we need to head, umm . . . south."

We reached the corner, crossed because the light was with us, and began to head south, or what I believed to be south, the lights and the other pedestrians around us wavering wildly.

We were silent for a while, concentrating on our walking skills, when Morgan said, "I wonder if Saint Patrick's is open."

"Huh?" I asked, still clinging to her arm and walking with my head down.

"Saint Patrick's. I wonder if it's open."

"You'd think it would be, wouldn't you? Sanctuary and all."

"I want to go inside," she said.

That was a surprising thing to hear her say, but at the same time it wasn't. Not at all. "We can go find out," I said. I had no real idea where we were at the time, what avenue, even. But what the hell? "What time is it?" I asked, holding out my arm so she could read my watch.

"A little before ten."

Not knowing what the time would have to do with anything, I said, "Let's take a peek."

At the next corner, we crossed the avenue again and doubled back the way we'd come.

"It's open," she said a few blocks later, "but it looks like they're getting ready to close up."

"Well, then . . . we should hurry."

She led me up the steps and through the massive open doors into the warmth. All my years in New York, I'd never been in St. Patrick's before. Never saw any real reason for it. In fact, the only New York church I'd ever been inside was one in my own neighborhood, and that was by accident. I'd been conned one Sunday morning into walking an old lady (who had no idea that I couldn't see) down an icy sidewalk. Then across the street to her church. Then inside the church and up the aisle to her seat in the front pew. After she took her seat, I fled, hoping I'd never run into her again.

As it is, I know very little about Catholic ritual, even though I was surrounded by Catholic kids growing up—and even after attending that mass twice in my teens. That's why I was surprised when Morgan, who had attended Catholic school, stopped by the votive stand. (I didn't even know it was called a "votive stand" until she told me.)

"Do you have some change?" she asked.

Thinking, drunkenly, that she meant the change I'd received after we paid for dinner earlier that evening, I reached into my pocket and slid my wallet out.

"No, no, no—I mean coins."

"Oh." I reached into the other pocket and pulled out a small handful of coins and handed them to her.

I heard them plink into a metal container, and then she pulled a candle off the display, where dozens of candles flickered. She lit the candle, then was silent for a moment.

Morgan isn't a religious woman—at least not in any traditional sense—but she lit the candle with an unmistakable reverence. There was no smirking irony about it at all. And somehow, when she did it, I understood.

"Who was that for?" I asked, as she took my arm to lead me farther inside.

"My grandma," she told me. "I could light one for your grandpa, too—the one you were close to."

"Oh, that's okay. I don't know how much he'd really appreciate it. But thanks."

Holding on to my arm, she led me up one of the side aisles, describing things as we went.

". . . and there are the big video monitors, and . . ."

There were a few other people in the cathedral that evening, but not many. Our footsteps, quiet as we tried to keep them, echoed around us. I could hear a few other hushed voices, but could see almost nothing at all. I was hoping I wouldn't trip and knock something over. A reliquary or something.

Morgan walked me to the altar, where we stopped and turned around, facing the cavernous interior.

"I wish you could see the organ up there," she whispered. "It's amazing.

150

This whole place is amazing . . . maybe you'd be able to see a little more of it if we stopped by in the daytime at some point?"

"We could do that. I'd like to see it."

She led me back down the center aisle, and I began to get a sense of the space around me. It's strange—if it's hushed the way St. Patrick's was that evening, you can still get a sense of the space around you, even if you can't see. It's almost as if you can hear the space, or feel it on your skin.

We reached the votive stand again, and headed for the doors. Just then, a man holding a broom came inside and stopped us.

"You have to take your hat off."

"Okay," I told him as I pulled it from my head. "No problem." I'd completely forgotten that it was up there.

Five steps later we were outside, and I put it back on, shrugging to no one in particular. Then we continued to look for a train.

I'm hardly a religious man. I wasn't touched by God while I was there that night. At least not the way I'd maybe been walloped by the Holy Spirit a few months earlier. But there was still something—something good and beautiful, even poignant—about stopping into St. Patrick's (and stopping into St. Patrick's all sloppy drunk) on a chilly autumn eve, about lighting a candle for a grandma who meant something to you, about just being there for a while. I don't know exactly what it was, but it was one of those brief, rare, good moments, like sitting in an old empty bar you'd never heard of or getting your feet wet in the ocean for the first time, that'll stick around for a while.

chapter eleven

S ince we started seeing each other, Morgan and I had always preferred to stick with home bars whenever possible. I mentioned that earlier. Bar-hoppers always annoyed us. Once we found a place that seemed to fit, we simply stayed there until something convinced us that it was time to move on. I was the same way with jobs and apartments, too.

It was never easy to find a bar with the proper vibe in the first place. A bar that was quiet, where the bartenders knew when to knock you, where everyone minded their own goddamn business and left us the hell alone.

A decent jukebox helps, too.

The way things tend to work in New York City, however, finding a home bar is always a temporary affair. It's all a matter of timing. Eventually, though, word about a quiet bar will get out, and it will suddenly cease to be quiet. The staff will move on, the youngsters will invade, the attitude will change. You can feel it happen, and when it does, it's time to leave.

Morgan and I were back at our most recent home bar—an open, airy place on a quiet side street, with a slate floor and a tin ceiling. Smaller tables lined the wall opposite the long wooden bar, and an enormous round table sat against the back wall. The picture windows in front meant that the bar was fairly bright during the daytime, but at night, except for a few scattered track lights, it was dark as sin.

It was fairly quiet during the day, most of the clientèle composed of Milano's regulars who'd either been eighty-sixed for a few days or were simply looking for a little change of pace. The bar was also home to a pair of cats, who'd taken a bit of a shine to us.

It was about eight o'clock. We were sitting at a little table pressed up against the wall, about halfway back from the front door, conspiring to snag an unclaimed bowl of peanuts over on the bar. It wasn't all that different from most any other night, but that was okay.

I was letting my eyes wander, exploring the darkness, without even thinking of seeing anything. Morgan called it my "Creepy Blind Stare." Then I saw a glow of white light.

Not a flash. It wasn't like someone had taken a picture and it wasn't like I'd been struck in the back of the head with a brick. It was a concentrated, steady white light that my eyes had panned over. I didn't know until I looked away that it had been there at all, and even then I thought it had probably been in my imagination. It took me a second to find it again, a second of roving the eyes back and forth, as if I were looking for a dropped spoon.

The table a few yards closer to the back and pressed up against the same wall we were next to was bathed in a pure, white glow. With the exception of the Jesus incident, I'd never seen anything like it before, and especially not in a bar like this one. When the light is bright enough, and it's within my extremely limited field of vision, I can still see with some clarity. Not the subtler details, but enough. And this was as if God Himself had cast a spear down from Heaven onto that singular spot for the sole purpose of allowing me—almost *forcing* me—to see something. Everything outside that ray of light was impenetrable and black. But inside, at that table, everything was clear.

That's what frightened me, because within that ray of light, sitting at that table, I found myself staring at . . . myself.

I don't much like to look in mirrors. (What's the point?) I don't take any great pride in my appearance. Still, I have some pretty solid notion of what I look like, and it was sitting a couple tables away, bathed in an ethereal white glow.

I tapped Morgan on the hand, leaned over, and asked her quietly, "I don't want to sound like a narcissistic pain in the ass or anything, and I know I can hardly see, but tell me—is that fellow sitting two tables away, um . . . me?"

I waited a second, trying to be nonchalant about it, took a swallow of beer, and tapped the cigarette in the ashtray, while she took a quick, furtive peek over her shoulder,

She turned back and leaned over to whisper, "Yes. Yes, he is."

"Thank you." It was, for some reason, a tremendous relief to hear that.

I stopped myself from running screaming from the bar, but the evening immediately took on a new strangeness. If I desired proof that everything I had ever perceived was an illusion of some kind, that everything I ever saw, felt, touched, or thought was part of some grand joke or cheap dream, this would just about do it for me.

A few friends joined him shortly afterward, and they all seemed to be having a pleasant time together. I kept stealing nervous glances over toward him in that otherworldly glow. I was trying to be as subtle as possible, but more than once, I thought I caught him staring back at me. It was obvious that he, too, had just seen something he didn't necessarily want to see.

Of course, he'd probably known from the beginning that this day would inevitably arrive, which was more than I could say.

With each glance, I tried to discover a detail that would give him away as a fraud. A mole, a brown tooth, huge, floppy ears. Unfortunately I couldn't see him in that sort of detail without moving closer. The glow shone like a halo about him, like the one surrounding Richard Lynch near the end of *God Told Me To.* If I got too close, it would probably burn me.

"His brow's a little heavier than yours," Morgan offered. "But the eyebrows are the same."

"So you're saying we're maybe dealing with the Cro-Magnon version?"

"But that's it, really. The brow. Everything else is in place."

"Great. But he doesn't have a hat. That's something, isn't it?"

"Actually . . . he does. He took it off earlier."

"Shit."

We—me and this other me—kept staring at each other with a mixture of curiosity, fear, and confusion. He from within the light, and me, as usual, in the darkness.

I started to test things out. I slowly raised my right arm to see if his left would go up. I discreetly moved the ashtray from one corner of the table to another to see if he'd do the same. I fired up my lighter and moved the flame in circles in front of me to see if he'd mimic my actions.

He did none of these things, of course, which left me looking like a jackass again.

The snow, which had been falling most of the day, had been replaced by a heavy rain, and for a few minutes, one of the most intense hailstorms I'd ever witnessed in New York. It came down solid, like a rain of BBs. Most everyone in the bar fell silent and watched, and listened. Then the hail stopped as abruptly as it had begun, and the rain returned.

A few years earlier, I had been on the F train on my way home from work when I overheard a sturdy young fellow who was pretending to be me, claiming to be the one who wrote "Slackjaw" every week, apparently in a misguided effort to pick up chicks.

Another time, another train, I saw myself twenty years in the future sitting across the aisle, and was mortified to discover that nothing had changed. Same hat, same long hair. Twenty years in the future, I was even still wearing the same goddamned shirt. The only thing that had changed was the fact that I seemed to have gained about forty pounds. But this was different. That youngster two tables away wasn't pretending to be me openly and shamelessly. This kid here, that night, was me. What's more, this time I had a witness. It wasn't just my paranoid buffoonery at work.

"We should go over and talk to him," Morgan suggested.

"Ohhh, I don't know about that . . . I mean, I pretty much already know what I think about most everything."

"Yeah, I guess you're right—and anyway, what would you say that wouldn't sound completely insane? 'Excuse me, sir, but are you me?' I don't think that would go over real well."

"Certainly not with most people, anyway. Plus there's that whole matter-antimatter problem. Y'know—*kaboom.*"

When we left the bar a couple of hours later, he was still sitting there with his friends, still having a good time. Before we stepped out the door, I gave me a long, hard stare, and he gave it right back.

The next night, he was back, but without the halo. And the night after that, too. It came so's we just expected him.

"You're here again," Morgan would tell me upon his arrival, or "You just walked in the door."

He had appeared out of a beam of white light and was now becoming a regular, as much as the old-timers like Victor or Jack or the Greek toy salesman or any of the other skells (or we) were regulars.

I never spoke a word to him and tried not to sit too close to him. Still, I began to wonder about what it was he did during the day. Was he up and out on the streets early every morning, running around the city, helping old ladies across the street, playing the lute for patients in the burn ward, taking the homeless out to lunch, romping with orphans, doing Good Deeds, while I spent my days avoiding phone calls, typing stupid stories about myself, plotting revenge, and stewing over past injustices? Probably. Then, after a day of good-deed-doing, he devises to meet up with me at the bar every night (in his own way) to draw energy from me, further depleting my already meager spiritual resources. I began to speculate idly if he had been somehow responsible for that rash of blackouts I'd had.

Then I simply assumed that he had.

It only took a few weeks of this sort of vampirism before Morgan and I decided that it was time to switch home bars again.

Sometimes it could seem like all Morgan and I did was sit in bars, talk with each other, and get drunk, but we did more than that. We gambled, too.

I've long held that on a philosophical level, gambling was among the purest of metaphors for day-to-day life condensed and made much more exciting. Every day was a risk. You never knew what was going to happen or where you'd end up, not really, yet you stepped outside and took your chances. Nothing at all might happen, or the subway tunnel might cave in around you. You might be shot in the leg by a stranger for no reason, or find a bag full of unmarked bills. Gambling—from office football pools to high-stakes poker tables—was an admission and celebration that you accept the fact. It symbolizes, in its own way, the eternal present, where the past and future lose all meaning and no longer exist. What matters is neither the last hand nor the next race—only what's in front of you at that moment.

That I'd always been an unbelievably unlucky gambler didn't matter. I knew as much, and I didn't let it bother me.

We each set aside some money over a few months, took a trip to Atlantic City, and lost it all in under twenty-four hours. Afterward, though we left with no regrets, we decided that maybe it would be wise to find something closer and cheaper. Luckily, we were within easy striking distance of both the Belmont and Aqueduct racetracks. Morgan had never been to the track before. I'd been going for years whenever I had the chance, and I had yet to place a winning bet. We were both long past due.

One Thursday in May of 1999, I made a phone call to the track and was assured by a kindly and excitable woman that the horses were, indeed, running all weekend, and that I should definitely come on down. So, the following Sunday morning, Morgan and I hooked up at the Jay Street–Borough Hall subway station in Brooklyn, hopped on an A train, and settled in for the ride.

I'd never been to Aqueduct before, and I wasn't exactly sure how to get to the track once we got off the train. I figured that since the stop was called "Aqueduct Racetrack," it couldn't be too hard. There would probably be signs.

"If it's not obvious," I told her, "if there are no signs or anything, we'll follow the other people who get off the train. We'll be fine." It was the old strategy that I'd been using for years to make people think I actually knew where the hell I was going.

"Ohh, I've heard that plan of yours before," Morgan countered doubtfully. "And it's never, ever worked."

160

"We'll see." Even if it had never worked before, I thought it was still a fine plan, as plans go.

As we rattled along, I told Morgan about the last time I went to the track, back when I still lived in Philly.

"I played hooky from work one day, " I began. "That was when I was a bill collector, and Grinch—Grinch was living in Philly then. He and I hopped on his bike and rode up to Philadelphia Park. It was a nice place, but nobody was there, the place was almost empty except for a few dozen weasely, greasy old guys in bad hats."

I paused a second, reconsidering the tone of that description.

"Now," I went on, "I've told you that, for all my years of trying, I've never won a race in my life, right? Years and years of trying, dozens of tracks, hundreds of races, and never, ever once have I picked a winner."

"Many times."

It was true, too. But even though I never won a dime at the track, I never lost all that much, either. Everything I put down, maybe, but that didn't amount to much. You didn't need nearly as much cash at the track as you did at a casino.

"Right. So, in the fifth race, I put a ten-dollar win bet down on this horse. I forget what his name was—I wish I could remember, but it's long gone. Odds weren't too bad. Anyway, they break out of the gate, right? And my horse takes the lead. I'd seen that happen too many times before, so I wasn't going to get too excited about it yet."

"Uh-huh?"

"His lead keeps getting bigger. He keeps pulling farther and farther ahead. It was incredible—it looked like I was actually going to win one. Never been done before, so it was very exciting."

"Yeah?"

"They're on the backstretch and my horse, whatever his name was—I wish I could remember it now—who had this fucking six-length lead, *stops.* Just *stops* dead in his tracks. Then he stands there, perfectly still. The jockey is looking around like he doesn't know what's going on, and the horse is watching all the other horses run past him. Once they're passed, he just flops over in the middle of the track, dead as can be. And Grinch, who was sitting next to me, he says, ''Hey, uh, looks like your horse just, uh, *died,* there, Slack.''"

"Oh, my God. Wha'd they do?"

"Oh, they brought out the big horse ambulance, loaded him up, and carted him away."

"Jesus."

"Yeah, and that was only the fifth race. In the very next race, none of the horses died, everything went fine. I lost, of course. My horse came in last, but it was a photo finish. When it was over, the track reviewed the results, and posted the winner, same as any other photo finish."

"But they posted the wrong one . . . ?"

"*Exactly.* Imagine a group of hundreds of old men, all of them thirty, forty years older than us and all of them *pissed,* standing up out of their seats,

cigars clamped between their teeth, shaking their fists in the air and screaming, 'You bastards! You cheated us! You sonsabitches!' It was damn near a
riot. These guys were out for blood."

"What happened? Did the track have to pay out both?"

"Yeah, both horses they had to pay out for. They lost a helluva lot of
money on that one race. In fact, it was in the newspaper the next day—the
fact that no fuck-up like that had happened at an East Coast track in over
thirty years. It really was almost a riot. A riot of broken old men with cigars."

Half an hour later, we reached our stop and got off the train. Sure
enough, we could see the track from the elevated platform—the enormous
white structure with the horses painted all over it. Simple as pie.

As might have been expected, hardly anyone else got off the train, and
those who did were at the far end of the platform, anyway, and they all vanished too quickly to follow. Once again, my plan to follow them was shot to
shit right off the bat. Thinking we'd just figure it out once we got down there,
we started heading toward the nearest exit, at the rear of the train. We hadn't
walked but a few steps when Morgan stopped short.

I tried to follow her gaze, squinting toward the exit, perhaps fifty feet
away. Two people, it looked like, were standing there, just inside the big nut-
grinder turnstile, waving at us and yelling. I couldn't decipher what they
were saying—their words were being whipped away by the wind.

Morgan took a few steps forward, then stopped again. I kept heading in
their direction, but she grabbed my arm.

"Wait," she said.

Then I heard a woman's voice slicing through the wind.

"Call the police!"

What do you do? If this scene were taking place in Green Bay, the answer would be simple. You would immediately find out what the problem was, see if there was anything you could do right there, then find a phone and call the police. But if you've lived in New York for a while, your immediate gut reaction to a situation like this is that it's a setup. You know that one of these people—or someone hiding in the shadows behind them—has a gun.

We took a few steps closer. The pair continued to yell. One was male, one was female. One of them was banging something metallic against the bars of the turnstile. We determined, as we got closer and could hear them more clearly, that they were trapped in there. They'd gone through the turnstile, went down a few steps, found the gate locked, and now couldn't get out.

(Or so they said.)

There was a public phone on the platform, so Morgan called 911 and explained the situation to the operator, who transferred her to the Transit Police. She explained it to them once again, and was told that someone would be there in a few minutes. After she hung up, we finally walked all the way down to the trapped couple, and only then saw that they were both in their sixties. They seemed harmless enough.

"We've been here for two hours," the man said.

"We were on our way to the racetrack, came this way, and got trapped," his wife explained again, still clinging to the padlock she'd been banging against the bars of the turnstile.

Two hours? How many trains must have gone by in two hours? How many people had ignored them?

"And I just had heart surgery," the wife told us, tapping her chest.

We assured them that help was on the way, then headed to the other end of the platform (where we'd be able to get out, we hoped) to make sure the token booth clerk knew what was going on. Then we had some races to catch. I looked at my watch. We still had half an hour before post time.

The clerk behind the bulletproof glass didn't seem too concerned about the situation. He had that doughy, wall-eyed look that made me think he wasn't quite right. He told us that he knew all about the couple up there, and that it would be taken care of, so we headed outside.

Just as we hit the sidewalk, a police cruiser pulled up and stopped. When the cop got out, we gave him a thumbnail sketch of the situation.

"They've been there for two hours," Morgan told him.

"Two hours, huh?" he said, then chuckled enigmatically before going inside. Did he know something we didn't? Regardless, now that someone was on top of it, we could head to the track, our consciences clear.

"Where do you suppose we go from here?" I asked. We looked around, and nothing was making itself obvious. No signs, no arrows. We couldn't even see the track anymore from where we stood, so I stepped back inside the train station to see if the token clerk might help us out. He worked here. He had to know.

"Excuse me?" I shouted through the glass. It wasn't like he was busy. "How do we get to the horses from here?"

"*Hor*-ses?" he asked.

Jesus, this guy really is retarded.

"Yeah, you know—the track? Aqueduct? What's the easiest way?"

"They haven't had any races there in quite a while."

"You're kidding."

"Not for a while now."

"But . . . I just talked to someone on Thursday who said that they were running today."

"Hey, go see for yourself, I don't care. Go through the gate and follow the path. See for yourself."

This can't be happening. I went back outside and told Morgan.

"Oh, he's retarded," she said. We climbed through the broken gate in the chain-link fence next to the station and started following a dirt path. Before long, the track rose into view, on the other side of an immense parking lot half-filled with cars.

"See? Look at all these cars. There's got to be something going on here." It was just past noon, first race was at twelve-thirty, and I was hoping she was right. Still, as we began to cut across the asphalt, things seemed strangely silent. There were no new people pulling into the lot, no one milling about outside, no noise at all leaking out through the open structure we were approaching. Only the occasional whistle of the wind.

We kept walking. As we were passing a group of parked cars, Morgan asked, "Why do you suppose all these cars have plastic wrapped around the seats?"

"And stickers in the window?" I added.

"And why are they all the same model?"

It took us slightly more than a second longer to realize that what we were crossing was a new-car lot.

"Well, *shit.*"

Undaunted by the revelation, we kept walking toward the track, thinking it was a fluke, that only a small portion of the lot was owned by a car dealership, and that all those other cars were owned by people who'd driven here to lay down some bets. We kept looking for anything that might prove the token clerk a liar and a retard.

"Look at all those satellite dishes," Morgan pointed out. "There's something going on here."

But when we got to the clubhouse entrance behind the satellite dishes, it was empty and locked.

"Maybe the club opens later," I offered.

We walked around to the main entrance, only to find the ticket windows locked and empty, too, the iron gates pulled down.

Why did that woman on the telephone lie to me?

We walked a few yards away to consider our options, and I pulled out a cigarette.

"Hmmm."

"Hmmm."

Out of nowhere a vision of hope appeared. A large, middle-aged Hispanic woman walked around the corner and pushed her way through one of the front gates, which turned out to be unlocked after all. Here was our angel.

We followed her inside. She stopped several yards in front of us, turned, and stared, an evil and frightened look in her eyes. She'd probably lived in the city long enough to be suspicious, too.

"Excuse me?" I called out to her, knowing better than to step any closer. She didn't move. "Hi, uhhh . . . are the horses, ah, running here today? By chance?"

She still didn't move, yelling back, "No! No horses! *No horses!* They all go away! To Belmont!"

Fucking Belmont.

Despite my defeated air, I waved a thank-you at her, and we retreated back through the door.

"Gosh, I'm real sorry about this," I said. "This is all very embarrassing."

"That's okay. Somehow this morning I had a feeling that things weren't going to turn out exactly the way we had planned."

"At least it's a nice day," I offered, grasping at straws.

"And at least we saved some old people—and weren't locked in a turnstile for two hours ourselves."

"I wonder if they're still coming over here after they get out?"

We stood there awhile more, looking around at the parking lot. I reached for another cigarette.

"Well."

"Hmmm . . ."

It looked as if the day was already shot at noon, until Morgan asked, "Wanna go see some monkeys?"

We walked back across the parking lot, back down the path and through the broken gate, kept our heads down to avoid eye contact as we passed the retard in the booth, and got on a train heading toward the Bronx, to go see some monkeys.

chapter
thirteen

It was early. Too early, really, but there I was with the rest of the too-early commuters trying to get out of Brooklyn at six-fifteen in the morning, all of us eager to get in to work. Maybe the rest of them, like me, were just trying to avoid the press of sweaty human flesh that would get under way sometime within the next half-hour.

It was an unusually chilly and overcast spring morning. The night before, I had visited a weekly open-mic night for recently released mental patients (though they told me they preferred to be known as "mental health consumers"), where I listened to them read their poems and stories and sing their songs and tell their jokes. I talked to a number of the participants as well, including the man who had organized it. My job today would involve turning it all into a coherent little story for next week's paper.

I was leaning back against the subway doors, looking down toward my battered black shoes, trying to take inventory of everything I needed to do once I got into the office. The doors opposite me opened at the Smith and Ninth Street stop.

Two kids got on—college kids from the sound of them. The bright, shadowless fluorescent lights of the subway car allowed me to see that one was tall, with a dirty blond ponytail and a thick neck. The other, smaller, dark-haired one was obviously the worshipful shadow. I heard them before I saw them.

". . . which I vomited forth in the bathroom at midnight, with the remnants of my last meal!" the tall one was bellowing, pompous and too loud for that hour.

The shadow was hawhawhawing himself beet-faced.

They sat down to my right, and the tall one continued.

"I went on to write, 'Human beings are simply vermin, and I feel obliged to say that because of my obviously superior intellect . . .'"

"Haw haw haw!"

"'. . . they muddle around like the grubs that they are in their own vomitus and filth!'"

"Haw haw haw!"

This went on for three stops, two loud, obnoxious college boys making fools of themselves by playing at misanthropy. Yeah, they hated people, boy did they. They were smarter than everyone else, they knew what the game was, and they were damned happy with themselves because of it. I stood against the doors thinking, *Yeah, I remember the first time I saw* Taxi Driver, *too.* Recognizing only then that I must've looked and sounded exactly like them when I was their age, I felt more than a little ashamed about it. At the same time, I stood there thinking, *Jesus, but I'm so sick to death of these young, cut-rate, dime-a-dozen "misanthropists."*

This was the first time I'd noticed that some sort of shift had occurred in my thinking. I may not have been what you'd call a Chipper Charlie, but I had come to realize that happiness was not as contemptible and shallow an emotion as I once took it to be. Whatever depths of generalized contempt for various strata of humanity I clung to—and there was plenty of that—I at least felt I'd properly earned and respected it.

Much of my rage these days arose from my own clumsiness, incompetence, and pride—the fact that I tended to run into more people on the sidewalk, on stairs, on subway platforms. These people couldn't really be blamed for that—especially when I didn't use my cane as often as I should—but part of me wanted to blame them, anyway. Even as I tried to explain and apologize after the fact, so many of them looked at me as if I were insane or drunk or merely stupid. They weren't listening. This enraged me. Even with the pills, sometimes my rage could be a dangerous and unpredictable animal, and because of that, I became very, very nervous and twitchy when dumped into a crowd. Perhaps not the best state of affairs for a "journalist," but there I was.

While there had been a time when I would scream and rant openly in public places, I now tried to keep any angry eruptions as quiet as possible. In New York, where a large part of the population, at least in the waning days of the twentieth century, preferred to think of themselves as misanthropists, what would be the point? Hundreds of thousands of people trying hard to prove how much they hate everything, trying to out-asshole each other and always failing. They ranted with smiles on their faces. They felt proud of themselves when they loudly proclaimed their disdain in public. Like these two kids on the train. It's a general rule I've discovered over the years—though I'm hardly the first to point it out—that the louder you are, the less there is to fear about you.

The night before, sitting in the small, crowded room that housed the psychiatric open mic, I hadn't felt all that nervous. In their own crazy way, the people who were there had shown me something.

"I wrote for thirty years," a small, wiry man with glasses and a heavy gray mustache told me at one point, "until I got sick. Then I stopped for ten years. Being a consumer can be a real drag."

They weren't loud, they didn't proclaim their insanity (except for occasional references to "getting sick"), they didn't celebrate it the way so many others (especially poets) tended to do. They didn't have to. They knew the real thing, and knew it was a pain in the ass. Instead, they were reasonable and kind, they encouraged each other. The fragile, monstrous egos you normally encounter at such things were nowhere to be found.

Time was—when I was a young man, when I talked like those kids on the train—I would've filled my article about the previous night with an endless string of nasty jibes about how nuts the whole event was. In spite of the months I'd spent in psych wards myself, I would've turned the tiniest tics I'd witnessed into spasmodic convulsions. I would've made fun of their "crazy" poetry and their "crazy" songs. I guess I just didn't feel like doing that any-more. Not to these folks, at least. They didn't deserve it.

After I left the receptionist's desk, one of the first stories that actually excited me involved interviewing the writer Harry Crews. Crews lived in Florida and wrote gritty, two-fisted novels about people—Southerners, mostly—who find themselves in uncommonly horrendous circumstances. He'd been through a lot himself, a hell of a lot more than I had. The face I saw on his book jackets and the voice I heard over the phone reflected that. Both were beaten and scarred.

I was a bit intimidated by the prospect of talking to him, even after some-one who had met him years before had warned me that he wasn't going to be what I expected. I'd heard stories. Former students of his described him as an angry, insane drunk. He had a reputation as a brawler and as perhaps not the most pleasant man you'd ever want to deal with. Still, after smoking half a pack of cigarettes, I screwed up my courage, picked up the phone, and dialed the number I'd been given.

When the first words Mr. Crews spoke to me, after I asked him an in-nocuous "How are you doing today?" were "I *hurt,*" I was certain I was going to be in for a long, uncomfortable afternoon. Interviews that start that way usually don't go very well.

Sure enough, I proceeded to ask all the wrong questions and make all the wrong points—like asking him very early in the interview why so many of his recent novels ended in exactly the same way (namely, with most of the main characters abruptly getting blown up somehow).

"Were you just getting bored or something?" I prodded. I was making, I thought, a lighthearted jibe, but he didn't take it that way. I probably wouldn't have, either, were I in his position. In later years, people would ask me similar questions about my own books, and I always had to fight off the urge to swat them.

"No, no, no . . ." he said, his ragged drawl sounding both a little saddened and a little annoyed. "I hope I wasn't getting bored. I hope I did it with a . . ." He sighed heavily and then fell silent.

I'm an idiot, I thought.

He didn't hang up on me at that point, which was a relief, as it would have left me with an unusually short interview. He just sighed a lot. He'd been through it before. Sighed, then kept talking.

"I mean, all fiction," he finally said, "is about the same thing: it's about people doing the best they can with what they got to do *with.* Sometimes with mercy, sometimes not. Sometimes with compassion, sometimes not. Honor, sometimes not. And so on."

I felt a breath of relief. I recognized what he was saying—he'd uttered the exact same words, in the exact same way, in the dozen or so other interviews I'd read. He may have slipped into reflexive, boilerplate interview mode, but at least he was talking again. I kept my mouth shut and listened.

"Hell, when I grew up in south Georgia, all the old people were at home. I learned my dialect at the knee of my granddaddy, and the stories he told. An old guy, an old woman, it doesn't matter if they've been to school or not. If they live to be sixty-five, seventy-five, ninety years old, they have seen all the ways that they can do. They've been around so many blocks, and they tell you stories about things. Knowledge turns to wisdom—to use some fancy kinda phrase that I don't too much care for, but anyway, I've said it and I'll stick with it . . ."

I knew that things were going to be okay, so long as I didn't blow it. Later in the interview, I asked him about his drinking. Crews had once been a famous, even outlandish, drinker, who had since stopped.

"I have been in three drunk rehabs," he told me. "They keep us for twenty-eight days. Didn't help me a damn bit. I tried to go to those meetings, but they just depressed the shit out of me. If you've heard one story about pissin' in an icebox when you're drunk, you've heard 'em all."

I've pissed in a lot of strange places, I thought, but didn't say, *but never in an icebox.*

"Only thing that worked for me—take one every morning, got it right by my toothbrush—is that I take six hundred fifty milligrams of Antabuse."

"Antabuse? Really?" That caught me by surprise. That was hard-core.

"You can't even *prescribe* that stuff in West Virginia, Virginia, a few other states. People *died* on this shit. One shot of alcohol, you won't even be able to talk when you get to the emergency room. So far as I know, I'm not suicidal, but there are a lot of things you've got to really be careful about. All kinds of that stuff you put on salads—salad dressing—there's desserts that they pour a thing of brandy over before they bring it to you. You have to check all that stuff, man. It's pretty potent."

"Jesus, huh?" I said, figuring it couldn't be misinterpreted.

"I wrote, somewhere, that the hardest job I ever had was being a drunk. I was a drunk for a long time. Ain't no other way to say it; I don't like 'alcoholic,' I like 'drunk,' because it sounds more like what it is."

"It's like that old Jackie Gleason joke," I offered, glad to be able to tell it to someone who would understand. "Alcoholics go to meetings." He laughed hard at that one, hard for a man who, as I understood it, rarely laughed, and it sounded good to hear.

"Yeah," Crews went on. "Jackie said that he drank for the ancient and honorable reason of getting totally schnockered. That's the way I am. I mean, if you've never seen an Indian drink, then you oughta watch me. I'd just pour it down. That's just the way it's been. But you know, I didn't start drinking till I was thirty years old. I didn't drink all the way through the Marine Corps. But when I started, well by God, y'know, I think I'd been an alcoholic all that time and didn't know it. I drank with both hands."

"What made you stop?"

"I had a choice," he replied. "I could write, or I could drink. But I couldn't do both."

"But you must've been both drinking and writing for a long time there," I pointed out. "You put a lot of books out."

"There's another thing. I think one of the reasons I became—and I've been sober now, God, for about ten years. I started drinking about thirty, and it didn't turn bad on me, against me, until I was about forty-six, forty-seven, maybe? And when it turned, it turned like a vicious dog, man—hell, I just *couldn't* drink. Nobody wanted to be around me and everything went to hell. I have to say, though, that if somebody had told me that I could've got it back together the way I did, I would've said, 'No way.' I live in a nice house—it's nice to me, at least. When you grow up in a tenant farmhouse, anything's nice. But it's in the woods and it's on a little creek, and I got myself a dog and everything's kinda cool."

Everything's kinda cool. That was another thing that worried me, though it remained unspoken. Despite my fears of being trapped by patterns and schedules and regimens, when you got right down to it, things were, yes, kinda cool. I had an amazing girlfriend, my brain was a little off, sure, but it was as stable as it was likely to ever be, and I had a job that paid okay for what amounted to very little effort on my part. I had books of my own coming out. Nothing compared to his, but still. Maybe I was blind, but I was dealing with it. Things were cool. It was a situation that was completely alien to me, after so many years of struggle. The adrenaline rushes I used to get from stealing, or breaking windows, or setting fires were gone—but I was replacing them with other things that were different, but just as good in their own way. But wherever I was, I was still a long way from the wisdom that Harry Crews was talking about.

Weeks after the fact, long after the story had run, even, it still was hard to know quite how to take my conversation with that weathered old bird. Most writers are complete bastards, I'll be the first to admit, which is why I generally tried to avoid their company, but Mr. Crews was all right. He'd been through hell, wrote and drank his way through it, and now, if not exactly "happy," he at least seemed satisfied and comfortable. But, as another tattered cliché goes, at what price?

There was a sad, unguarded moment during the interview, when he said something that I knew would stick with me. He had more than a dozen novels behind him, and I asked him if he ever went back and read them anymore. He said he did, though not often. That he still found parts of them very funny. "But you know," he said, wistfully, "I always thought that I'd be better than I am."

It was true in my case, too, on any number of levels. I never planned on becoming a writer, but once it became clear that's what was happening, I always figured, like he said, that I'd be better at it. Maybe not great, but good at least. In the end, I saw myself as little more than a mediocre hack, but I'd come to be satisfied with that. I could want to be better at what I did, I could try to be better, certainly. That was the goal. But if I wasn't in the end? Eh, I was fine with that. I might've been lazy, but I was having fun.

When I looked at the other writers around me early on, when I was just getting started and was still full of the angry hubris of youth, I thought they were all crap. Other writers in the same Philadelphia weekly I was writing for, or in magazines, or in books—from pulp novels to bestsellers to classics—all of them crap. I was absolutely convinced that I could write rings around any of them, reduce them all to ashes. I was sure at the time that I was going to be the next Henry Miller, and so as a result, I grew enraged if I was ever criticized or edited.

As it turns out, I didn't become Henry Miller, and I learned that a good editor is an indispensable person to have on your side. And when I think about my own writing and compare it to the work of other authors, the poles have shifted. Today, even while listening to an audiobook of the sleaziest thriller or horror novel, more often than not I'll find myself thinking, "Man, this guy's so much better than me." And when I listen to a great work of literature, I'm simply flabbergasted, wondering in awe where in the hell these words could have come from.

Along similar lines, I guess I thought I'd be a better person, too. After all the terrible things I had done and said and written, suddenly, and for reasons I still wasn't exactly clear on, I just wanted to be more decent.

In this world, repellent as it can be, it only made sense. There were too many shits around as it was—both those people who were unconsciously shitty to everyone around them, and those (like those kids on the subway) who were trying really, really hard. I had spent too many years wallowing in misery and consumed with hatred. I knew how hard it was to claw yourself out of that, to catch even a quick breath of something peaceful along the way. I was thinking now that there was not much point in adding to the piles of misery everyone else already had to deal with.

It's not that I liked people any more than I ever had. I didn't, and I still tended to avoid them as much as possible. I was simply much less interested in going to the effort of making their lives worse than they already were.

In most cases, anyway. There are a few people out there who fully deserve a little extra misery. The cell-phone shriekers who careen more blindly than I do, so wrapped up as they are in explaining (loudly) to whoever's on the other end that they're "between Twenty-third and Twenty-fourth," those people who find it necessary to stick their elbows out as they're walking down the sidewalk, joggers, the smug.

Lord knows I still had evil thoughts. They came to me in flashes—if I see someone hobbling down the street in a walking cast and a surgical boot, the first thing I want to do is stomp on their foot. I was still tempted to knee people in the kidneys for no good reason on the subway. The trick is, I guess, not acting on these impulses.

"Yeah," Morgan asked me when I brought this up, "but for how long?"

Crews' line, "I always thought that I'd be better than I am," was less than an afterthought on his part, yet it hung around, reminding me in quiet moments of all the things I had forsaken. Self-pity wasn't the answer, however. Self-pity never was. It made things all the more pathetic and unbearable. Better to do something about it.

I began looking for little proofs, evidence that, despite all the things that seemed to be going so right, I hadn't lost everything in the process. That, de-spite everything—the eyes, the happiness, the small level of success that I had encountered—I hadn't grown weak.

It was a stupid problem, but a common one. Much of what I'd achieved, at least in terms of books and the stories, was based on the fact that I was a snotty, hate-filled little asshole who did terrible things, both to himself and others. Now that I didn't feel that way anymore, what would become of me? Would I lose it all now? I guess I'd find out.

As it happens, not long after I started thinking about all this, I received a note from Grinch.

Jim, it began.

I wear tailored Donna Karan suits. I have a Hugh Grant haircut. I've got $500 designer glasses sitting on my nose.

I am always going into high-zoot restaurants, schmoozing with celebrity chefs and cutting $$$ deals. I am constantly on the cell phone, usually to Italy or France, yelling to people about euro exchange rates and container-sized shipments of wine. I lift weights all the time, and run 50 miles a week. This regime has given me a 32-inch waist and a size 43 jacket.

Jim, how do you think people on the street react to my apparent success, sartorial splendor, and youthful good looks?

That's right, they try to physically attack me. Upon first sight of me, oth-erwise respectable-looking citizens spontaneously erupt into a violent rage.

I am a walking lightning rod for resentment. I'm still at it. I'm out in the streets, extracting, distilling, and amplifying all the hatred and vileness in people's hearts. Some things never change.

Keep on ruining it for everybody,
Grinch

While I had, over the previous few years, found myself baffled by Grinch's celebration of all that was upscale and suburban given where we'd both come from, I guess I should have known that he was one of the few people who could in real day-to-day life (and not just the movies) transform the suburban into the honestly Satanic. In Grinch's case, it went far beyond an issue of making a pilgrimage to the Crossroads. There was no need for him to do anything like that, given that I was fully convinced he was one of Beelzebub's nephews to begin with. There was something about him that would never be destroyed, an electric wickedness that allowed him to be gleefully sadistic in any situation and get away with it. He was still the truest of pure sociopaths. No, Grinch would never lose in this world.

chapter fourteen

I try to make a point of avoiding "literary" happenings—book parties and the like. I try to avoid any kind of party, to be honest, but book parties in particular. So often they turn out to be intolerably arid roomfuls of sophisticated hobnobbery. The idea of hobnobbing with sophisticates is one I don't particularly relish. I've never been a sophisticate, not by a long shot, and have very little to share with people who are.

I now had the option of isolating myself. Before there had been no option—in the lean years, I was simply isolated most of the time. I locked myself in the apartment and drank, and that was fine. Even when I was a kid, I had chosen to spend much of my time alone, reading or watching movies.

It was those early steps outside the house, when I first began meeting the general public on their own terms, that I realized I didn't care much for them.

Most of the jobs I'd had over the years—bookseller, museum guard, bill collector, receptionist—involved dealing with the public in a very intensive manner, and that only confirmed my initial notions.

Now, however, I had a choice. For the most part, I dealt only with those people I chose to deal with. Although Morgan and I spent a lot of our time in public places, we carefully chose places we knew would be quiet, and where we wouldn't be bothered.

Thinking about it, it's quite possible that it was that choice—the choice not to interact with people if I didn't feel like it (and I rarely did)—that was a major contributing factor to this new way of thinking, and to my increased happiness.

I think it's true of most anyone—if you're forced to confront the public on a one-to-one basis for several hours a day every day, you're going to want to hurt them.

Now, after the books and the column and the mild attention both had foisted upon me (I'd even been put on the television once), I could probably go to fabulous parties and nightclubs if I wanted to, but now more than ever, I didn't want to. The very idea made me queasy.

I knew plenty of writers—especially the younger ones—who craved that sort of attention, who did everything they could to get a little publicity and recognition. A mention in the gossip columns of the *Post* or the *Daily News* or *New York* magazine. They went out to all the parties and gave readings whenever and wherever they could, just to hear the applause and the fawning praise. I assumed that most of them, at heart, always wanted to be rock stars, and this is about as close as they were going to get. There's nothing wrong with that, I suppose. In my case, however, I've always preferred the anonymity of a dark bar or my apartment. I didn't even like having my picture taken. Steals the soul, don't you know.

But that's beside the point.

As with everything, I made certain exceptions. A good friend of ours whom we'd met through the paper, Bill Monahan was his name, had just published his first novel, and it was a good one. When he invited me and Morgan to his book-release party in Manhattan, we told him we'd be there, despite our (or at least my) reservations concerning such things. I would put them behind me for an evening. Morgan in general was as hesitant about crowds and parties as I was, but in cases like this—which would provide us the opportunity to see some people we hadn't seen in a long time—we decided it would be worth it. We liked Bill a lot, and we wanted to show our support. Nothing wrong with that.

We met up after work, grabbed a quick dinner, then headed up to Midtown again.

I'm told that the Carnegie Club on West Fifty-sixth Street is quite the elegant joint. Couldn't see any of it myself, but Morgan described it in detail as she maneuvered me through the early crowd toward the back, first to say hello to Bill, who was talking with his agent, then to sit down in a dim, comfortable corner booth with a couple of beers we'd picked up along the way.

"Y'know," I said, apropos of nothing, "people are always asking me why I don't get a Seeing Eye dog. You've heard most of the reasons already—the cats, the size of the apartment, having to walk the damn thing twice a day."

"Right," said Morgan.

"It came to me one day last week on my way to work. I was walking down Twenty-third, the way I always do, and I passed by the Associated Blind Building, the way I always do." (The Associated Blind is an apartment complex designed specifically for the visually impaired.)

"Uh-huh?"

"And, just like every morning, I see all these people coming out of there with their guide dogs. Then it suddenly hit me. You know what I've *really* got against Seeing Eye dogs?"

"I'm waiting."

"The fact that they're so *defeated*. They're just broken creatures. They aren't real dogs anymore. They aren't stupidly joyous the way dogs are supposed to be. They aren't hopping all around, yapping at birds, sniffing other dogs. They're just plodding along, hopeless as anybody. All their dogness has been trained out of them."

"Yeah—they're like meat robots."

"Exactly." Moments like that clarify for me once again why Morgan and I get along so well. I could talk to her about anything, and I knew she'd get it.

We were soon joined by a young woman named Jane, a friend of Bill's who had also once worked at the paper. She was in her mid-twenties, but I didn't hold it against her. She was a bright woman.

So we sat in the comfy velvet-lined booth, and talked, and drank.

As the crowd grew thicker, I started hearing the pointedly dropped names of a few of the luminaries who were in attendance. The entire "Page Six" crew of gossip columnists from the *Post* was there, it seemed. Magazine writers and young novelists I'd never read, other publishing-industry types I'd never heard of, but who were supposed to be important people. Nobody I was particularly interested in talking to. It was a very healthy turnout, and regardless of how nervous I get in crowds—most notably in crowds of people like this—I was happy for Bill. It seemed to be quite the wingy-dingy, as my mom would call it.

We stayed in the corner, talking, drinking some more. Every once in a while, someone would go to the bar and bring back another round. It was all okay.

At one point, however, around eight o'clock, two interlopers appeared. Gatecrashers, it would seem, taking advantage of the open bar and the elegant crowd.

I have no problem with gatecrashing on principle, having learned to survive that way myself when I'd had nothing else. While I was doing it, however, I also learned the two most important lessons of professional interloping: do not, if at all possible, call attention to yourself, and, most important, do not be an asshole (unless, of course, that's your goal).

They were rules I had forsaken on a number of occasions, lord knows—within the past couple of years, even—but this was different. This time I was on the other side, if only accidentally.

These two apparently hadn't learned those fundamental rules yet, as they began hitting on Jane in an unpleasant, unwelcome, and wholly unimaginative manner.

"You know," I heard one of them say, "you have every physical attribute that I'm looking for in a woman. You're really *hot.*"

Jane asked them, too politely I thought, to leave, explaining that she wasn't interested and already had a boyfriend. Much to our surprise, they went away, if briefly, only to return a few short minutes later, their drinks freshened (that's what sophisticates do, isn't it? "Freshen" things?) in order to continue with their foul boorishness.

"You know," one of them said as they stood in front of Jane once again, not five feet away from where Morgan and I were sitting and listening, "you really turn me on."

Jesus. I've been in a lot of low-class bars in my time, heard a lot of sloppy and hopeless pickup lines, but at least most of the drunks who'd tried them, hopeless as they were, had made an attempt to be clever.

Having heard more than enough by now, Jane finally stood, stepped around them, and left.

When she did this, the interlopers assumed her place, settling themselves into the velvet-lined booth with us.

That simply wasn't the thing to do.

"So," Morgan asked them, after it was apparent that they intended to stay there with us for a while, "where are you from?"

I could tell by the tone of her voice, the sharp, mild quaver running just beneath the surface, what she was up to. Socratize them into a corner; get them to admit that they didn't belong at this particular private party, let alone in this booth with us. Then, with luck, get them to leave for good. We'd been having a fine time chatting with Jane, until these two destroyed that. Now it was our turn.

"I'm from Woodstock," the one nearest me admitted. I couldn't see him, but from his voice it sounded like he was just a kid. I'd learn later that he was much older, but at the time he sounded to be in his twenties. And *smug*. Oozing with what Morgan calls a "sense of entitlement."

"Yeah? And what do you do?" she continued.

He said he was part of a writer's group. Or rather, "writer's group." That's never good news. I don't even know what those are, but they sound pretty awful. His friend, we were told, was "in media," whatever the hell that might mean. It probably meant that he was an ad salesman. Or a television repairman. Or a paperboy.

(Again, I no longer carried with me the generalized contempt I once did, but there was no denying that some people simply deserve it.)

"And what are you doing here?" she pressed. There was silence from the other side of the booth.

"Are you friends of the author's?" They hemmed and hawed a bit, finally admitting that no, no they weren't.

"So," I jumped in, "do you happen to know who this party's for?"

Morgan's a much more subtle player at these things than I am.

190

"Sure," the smug one nearest me answered, offering nothing further.

"Uh-huh." I said. Then the final question: "What's his name?"

There was another moment of silence—too long—before the smug one said, "Ummm . . ."

"Very good!" I applauded. I leaned in toward him and said, "Look, son, why don't you just skedaddle?"

"I'm sitting here enjoying my drink." he replied

"Yeah, but we don't *want* you sitting here with us. Please go someplace else to enjoy your drink." I thought I was being polite, but firm. He just couldn't take the hint (which, come to think of it, wasn't a "hint" at all).

"I'm just sitting here, enjoying my drink," he repeated. He was so smug, so self-satisfied and arrogant. It was infuriating, and I could feel the tightness in my skull, the initial bad tremors begin to tingle down my arms and my spine again.

"C'mon, son, blow. Dangle." I made with a gesture. Then, realizing they might not understand what I was saying, reworded it more simply. "Son, get the hell out of here." He didn't move. He took a dainty sip of his martini (martinis in the hands of the young lead to nothing but trouble). Then he leaned back in his seat, crossed his legs, and *smirked*.

Well, that was it. Morgan finally couldn't take it anymore. First the way he was harassing Jane, now this. She stood up and, in a move that could probably, in military terminology, be called "escalation" (but certainly justified escalation), slapped the free martini out of his hand. In the darkness, I heard the smash and tinkle of glass on the tabletop, the light splash of vermouth and gin. She's got the guts and the fire, I'll tell you that—and I loved her for it.

The smug little son of a bitch jumped to his feet—I thought at first to brush off his pants—but instead, he took a swing at her.

It may have been an ineffectual slap, from what she told me later, but it didn't matter. That shit simply is not done.

Before I knew what was happening, the brain let loose, and I was kneeling on top of him, my hands around his throat, squeezing hard.

I didn't stop to think that we were at a fancy book party in a fancy club full of fancy people, and that perhaps killing somebody wasn't appropriate. I didn't stop to think (until later) that it was a good thing I didn't end up grabbing a seat cushion instead of his throat, which would just've been embarrassing. In that instant after he took the swing at Morgan, I listened to where that annoying voice of his was coming from, and aimed a tad south. All I could think about as I knelt atop him was what he had done and what a soft, tiny neck he had. I knew that if I kept squeezing it the way I was, my fingers would come to meet in the middle, kind of like squeezing a half-filled balloon.

Then it was over. A few brief moments after it had started, I was pulled off him, and he rolled away from beneath me. I'm not sure what happened, but suddenly I was sitting back in my seat again, and he was standing on the other side of the table, out of reach, his collar askew.

"I'm gonna go get the police and press charges!" he shouted, loud enough for everyone to hear. "That was *assault*!"

"Yeah? Go ahead," Morgan, sitting next to me, told him.

"I will!"

"Good. Go ahead."

"I will!"

But he didn't. Funny, but as I sat there, feeling perfectly calm now, relaxed, cleansed even, part of me was thinking that perhaps she shouldn't encourage him this way, and part of me was hoping he would indeed go get the cops. I was curious to hear what he would tell them. Especially after I whipped out the red-tipped cane.

"So," the officer would ask him, after taking down his story, "you were beat up by a blind man after you tried to hit a woman?"

Soon, there were others there around us, drawn by the whiny shouts. Our friend Sam—a former editor at the *Press*—was on the scene first, soon to be joined by several other people, and the interloper was explaining to them all that he'd done nothing, was just sitting there, quietly enjoying his drink, when I started strangling him for no reason whatsoever. Nobody seemed to believe him very much.

He and his friend were asked to leave by forces more persuasive than we had been, and eventually they did.

Morgan and I got a couple more beers. We were both a bit worried that the brief incident might put some sort of damper on Bill's party—it was his party, after all—but we were assured that everything was cool. Most of the people in the crowded room, it turned out, including Bill, were never even aware of what had happened in that dark corner until days later.

You simply don't do the things that kid was doing and expect to get away with it. Not where I come from, at least. I know people do, especially in a town like New York, and I know that I spent years getting away with things like that myself, but you shouldn't expect to. That's the point. Unfortunately, the people who do those sorts of things merit much worse than they usually get. For once, I'd actually ruined things for someone who deserved it.

I t was a long-held theory of mine that almost all bars are great on Sunday afternoons, but nightmares on Thursday and Friday nights. There was one Brooklyn bar just a few blocks from my apartment that had always been a particularly fine place in which to waste a Sunday afternoon, so that's where Morgan and I were, and that's what we were doing.

It was an old Irish place called The Portal, which was basic, but lovely. Beautiful woodwork, a fine beer selection, a half-decent jukebox, and a welcoming vibe. They even had a dart board in the back room—an increasingly rare amenity in most New York bars, and one I found it best to avoid. We'd never had any troubles there, and the bartenders were always friendly and generous.

We were feeling a mite peckish, and The Portal didn't serve food (none of the places we went to did), so Morgan and I picked up a couple of sandwiches on the way, then showed up at the bar about ten minutes after the doors were unlocked. Got a first round, then took a table in the back.

The sun was out, but the wind remained irksome that afternoon. I'd been locked in my apartment for the past four or five days, sitting cross-legged on a broken chair in front of a computer. My head hurt, my legs were numb, and my back had become a spasmodical wonderland. I knew I had to replenish myself with beer and some amiable human contact before I went all funny—or funnier—in the head.

It was working, too. The quivery stress was ebbing, the pain barely noticeable anymore. We were speculating idly about friends we hadn't seen for a while, and joking about some horrific crimes we'd heard about on the news that week. By two o'clock, the sandwiches were a pleasant memory, the inevitable "post-pastrami daze" that followed was beginning to fade, and we were nearing the end of our third round.

A few more people had come in and were now crowded around the taps. One woman was holding a tiny dog in her arms.

When it came time to go get the fourth round, I hesitated. When the bar is empty and the sun is shining through the front windows, I'm usually able to maneuver my way around the silhouettes of chairs and tables in order to get refills, then return them to the table without incident. When there are people afoot, however, and they've been reduced to two dimensions in my eyes while remaining three-dimensional in everybody else's, well, that's when I have trouble. Morgan, as a result, is forced to do most of the running. I'd gone up for the last round, but now with the crowd around the taps much larger and more mobile, I knew I'd have a bad time of it and would probably spill too much on the way back.

"Umm . . ." I said to Morgan, "could I ask you a favor?"

"Of course you can," she said, taking the glasses and heading toward the bar. I pulled a cigarette from my pocket and lit it.

When she returned a few minutes later, she was smiling. As she set the fresh pint in front of me, she whispered, "The other you is here."

"Oh, you're kidding."

I didn't need to ask her what the hell she meant. I knew. It had been a long time, but I guess I expected it one of these days. I was just sorry it had to happen here, in Brooklyn no less, at one of the taverns we had adopted as our home bar after fleeing the one where he had first materialized. If he decided to occupy this place, too, I wasn't sure where we'd go next.

"The woman holding the dog?" Morgan said. "He's with her."

"Great."

Worse, moments after she told me all this, the man, woman, and dog sat down at a table just a few feet away from us. Like he always did.

"He's bleached his hair," Morgan whispered so they wouldn't hear.

It's a start, I thought. Of course, it may have only been a side effect from spending so much time bathed in God's Holy Light. Damn him, anyhow.

Fortunately or unfortunately, there was no beam of light on him this afternoon. And given the nature of the natural light in the bar, I couldn't see him at all. I just had to take Morgan's word on things.

"He still looks exactly like you," she said. "Apart from the hair."

"Is he wearing his hat today?" I asked, still worried.

"No, no hat."

"And his brow's still a little heavier than mine, right?"

She looked. "Yeah. A little bit. He eyes are more deeply set."

That was always hard to imagine, actually, given that I once had a German photographer make reference to my "apelike" brow.

Like the last place, this bar also had a resident cat, which is something I always like to see in a bar—though this one was hiding somewhere at the moment. When the woman who was with the Other Me unchained her small bulldog, the first thing it did was click briskly over to the cat's food dish, which rested on the floor beneath the jukebox. It sniffed the food, then turned and clicked back to the table. It was one of those dogs that never stopped moving.

Moments later, the dog returned to the cat's dish, this time dipping its head and, in an instant, devouring all the food that was there. Then it moved on to the water dish, and neatly finished that off, too.

Neither the woman nor the Other Me said a word about it. They seemed to think it was cute or something.

"So much for going around doing good deeds," Morgan noted. "Now he seems like kind of an asshole."

"Yeah," I agreed, glad to hear it, "a real *jerk.*"

The room, as they say, became rationalized in that moment, as all the details started coming together.

Bleached hair? Bleached blond hair on a man is almost never a good idea, even if the man in question is Klaus Kinski. The roving-dog business, too—if Jesus could set a herd of pigs (demon-possessed or not) charging off a cliff into the sea, then this guy, blessed as he had apparently been at one point, could certainly deter a dog from eating the food of an innocent bar cat. What's more, his beam of heavenly light was missing.

"It wasn't a beam of heavenly light," Morgan said. "He was sitting in front of a window."

"No, no—I'm pretty sure it was a beam of heavenly light. Straight from God."

"It was just the light coming through the window."

"But the first time we saw him it was night."

"No, it wasn't."

I insisted, however. There's no denying that the beam of light had been there that first time we saw him. And now it was gone. What could it mean? Had he fallen from grace?

I'm fully aware that, for most people, having it pointed out that some stranger looked just like them would merit little more than an "Imagine that." Possibly grist for a brief mention over the dinner table that evening, but nothing more, and soon forgotten. So what was so different here?

Well, first of all, there was that spear of light direct from God's hand. Way I see it, he was sent down here on a mission to do Good Deeds, possibly in order to show me up. In order to do his job to the fullest, he had to stop by the bar every night to suck the life force from me. After we deserted the first bar, he'd lost track of me and, hence, his energy supply. Not long afterward, he'd gotten bored with goodness, and chosen instead to dedicate himself to rampant assholery.

Maybe there was a point there, a juncture within the past few months or years, when the Other Me signed his own contract, and we switched places. I wasn't out there doing Good Deeds, exactly, but I wasn't bleaching my damned hair and letting my dog run around all willy-nilly, either.

As before, I never spoke a word to him as we shared the back of the bar that afternoon. I did a lot of obvious squinting, perhaps, and Morgan and I did a lot of wild speculating, but I never confronted him. Part of me was curious, but ultimately I saw no reason for it. What would it have accomplished? Even if there was no massive matter-antimatter implosion, I might've come away with a nasty burn. All I know is that, when he and the woman and the dog left the bar, I wasn't feeling like the victim of some heinous ectoplasmic theft, the way I had in the early days.

I wonder if he was.

The question of "selling out" had always been a tricky one for me. When Grinch and I were performing as The Pain Amplifiers, we agreed early on that we would sell out, and sell out cheap, the first chance we got. Some major corporation wanted us to plug their new health drink, air freshener, or car stereo system, well, by God, we'd do it.

That opportunity never much presented itself. Mostly audiences threw things at us, and club owners asked us to go away.

That's the way I figured things would work with the writing as well. Most people would either be hostile or simply not care, and so the issue of selling out would never come up. And if it did, by chance, I would avoid it. Everything I had, I figured, meager as it was, I had because I was a cranky drunken bum, and that's the way I intended to keep it.

As the great Sterling Hayden once put it, "To be truly challenging, a voyage, like a life, must rest on a firm foundation of financial unrest. If you are contemplating a voyage, and you have the means, abandon the venture until your fortunes change. Only then will you know what the sea is all about."

I kept that in mind when, while I was still working as the paper's reception-ist, a man offered me a job doing voice-overs on television commercials for adult diapers.

"You have just the voice we're looking for," he said.

"Oh, I don't think I want to be doing anything like that," I told him, even though I could've used the money.

Seconds after hanging up the phone, I realized how twisted and funny it would've been, and I kicked myself for not taking him up on it.

Likewise, I hesitated for years before finally deciding that writing books maybe wouldn't be such an awful cop-out after all.

I wasn't even sure if I knew what "selling out" would mean in my case. Even if it had nothing to do with money, even if I didn't become a pitchman for adult diapers, would it still be selling out if I stopped writing about being poor and mean and drunk? I remember when I was young, picking up al-bums by my favorite musical acts and being sorely disappointed when the new album didn't sound exactly like the last one—if they suddenly decided to move into a reggae period, or become an electronic dance band. The same was true with my favorite authors and filmmakers. I wanted them to stay the same as they always were. I didn't need another Orson Welles documentary about a small Mexican boy and his donkey, or Hubert Selby going all sappy.

That feeling changed as I grew older, and I came to appreciate people who could evolve. Maybe I still didn't care for those who evolved into electronic dance bands or got hooked on astrology, but that's just me. Those writers, filmmakers, musical acts who did exactly the same thing time after time after time because "that's what the people wanted" not only began to bore me—they also made me sad. That seemed like more of a sellout than anything.

The idea—and that line from Sterling Hayden—did rise up again after I wrote that first book, and then was sent out on a ten-city tour to promote it. Putting a blind man on a cross-country tour was bad enough, I thought, but the day I thought it was all over, the day I was supposed to go home to Brooklyn and Morgan and the cats, I received a call from my publicist informing me that I had to make one more stop. Instead of flying home from San Francisco that afternoon, I had to hop on a plane that would take me to Los Angeles.

I had been out to L.A. a few times to see relatives when I was a kid, and I'd had a grand time. We went to Universal Studios and Knott's Berry Farm and the beach. Most recently, I had been there in the late eighties, and that time I saw with adult eyes what it really looked and felt like, what a horrible, wretched, empty stinkhole it was. One of the ugliest places on the planet. I had no desire to go back there ever again for any reason—and especially not now, when all I wanted to do was go home and sleep.

The reason for the extra stop, I was told, was that some television producers wanted to talk to me about turning the book into a television series. My gorge rose at the thought, but I agreed to see them, anyway. It seems I had little choice in the matter.

The meeting, I was informed after I arrived at LAX and was picked up by Mr. Wilson—a professional author escort and fellow former Wisconsinite—was to take place at the House of Blues. The House of Blues is a kind of Disneyland of blues and jazz, an enormous club in downtown L.A. that had been founded by a once-funny comedian.

It took nearly an hour to drive there from the airport. I was sweating, feeling scratchy and exhausted and unwashed. I needed a drink. The "scenery" didn't help. I loved movies, but God how I hated everything that went into making them.

Mr. Wilson pulled the car into a small parking lot behind the club, and we went in the back way. Once inside, we were directed to an upstairs lounge.

The room was windowless and unlit, so I could see nothing. I was led over to a couch, where I sat and immediately began feeling around the low table-top in front of me.

"The producers will be here in a second," Mr. Wilson told me. "They're in a meeting in the next room . . . uh, what are you looking for?"

"Ashtray," I replied, all my concentration focused on the search.

He reminded me that since I'd last visited Los Angeles, the city had succumbed to the anti-smoking whiners, and I worried again about the future of the country.

"Shit," I said.

"Can I get you anything else?"

"I could really use a beer."

"I'm afraid the bar's closed." It was four in the afternoon.

"So I can't have a smoke, and I can't have a beer? Jesus Christ, I think I'm beginning to understand why they call this the House of Blues."

Just then, the two producers entered the room. They weren't what I had imagined at all. Young men in their twenties who, from what I could tell in the darkness, were wearing white Nehru jackets.

"Can we get you anything before we start?" one of them asked. They certainly seemed friendly enough.

"Beer, please," I said, figuring that pushing for the ashtray would be pointless. I'd take what I could get. Much to my surprise, they got me one, though it took a while. I decided I would hear them out.

After they settled in on the couch across from me, they began, as I guess these things are supposed to, by heaping mountains of steaming, absurd praise on the book I'd written. I raised a hand to stop them.

"Look," I said, "there's no need to blow all this sunshine up my ass. I'm here. Just tell me what you'd like to do."

They weren't really sure, it seemed. A television series, they knew that much. A series that maybe I would write. That was something I wasn't interested in in the least, and I let them know as much. I was generally opposed to the whole idea, in fact, knowing just how badly they would fuck things up (if only because things like this were *always* fucked up). But I'd hear them out, because I'd said I would.

"But it wouldn't be softened up at all," one of them assured me.

"No," agreed the other. "It'll be real cutting-edge . . . just like that *Ally McBeal* show."

I nearly did a spit take, but I didn't want to waste the beer. *Ally McBeal* was a television series that was very popular at the time, concerning a young, sexually frustrated female lawyer working at a law firm populated with nothing but young, attractive, sexually frustrated lawyers. That's when I stopped listening. I was polite for the next two hours—especially when I was given another beer—but I was not listening. I'd heard enough.

When it was over, I stood, shook hands with both of them, and said, "We'll see."

On the way back to the airport, I commented to Mr. Wilson, "Y'know, if they make this show, and it's a piece of shit, I'd be ruined. And if they make this show, and it's great, and it's a huge hit . . . I'd be ruined."

When I felt guilty about making a little extra money by writing books, I remembered two things. First, I remembered that I wasn't making a whole lot of money. I wasn't getting one of those million-dollar advances you hear about. It was pretty pitiful, really, especially by New York standards, but still more than I had ever made before.

I also remembered the old, bad days, of saltines and tap water and three-dollar gallons of wine from countries I'd never heard of, of selling my plasma until I was sick, of being a paid medical-research subject at a place called the

Pain Research Institute, of worrying about the rent and if I'd be able to feed the cats. Sterling Hayden aside, I'd certainly spent a lot of time there, and there wasn't a goddamn romantic thing about it.

Of course the television money would have been nice, but I just couldn't do it—not after that *Ally McBeal* reference. And that adult-diaper money would've been nice, too, but as it was, Morgan and I got along just fine. We weren't extravagant people. Between us we had enough to eat okay, sit at the bars, go to the track every once in a while, feed the cats, and maybe one other thing.

chapter seventeen

I t was a Thursday in early September. Just about ten years to the week since my very first visit. The end-of-summer heat of the past weeks had finally cracked, and I was feeling far too tired for my years.

The previous night, I had slept for the first time in three days. Don't know why I couldn't sleep before that—maybe the heat, maybe the change of seasons or the full moon. Maybe sunspots. An awful lot of things can be blamed on sunspots. I finally did sleep, however, and awoke for the first time in a long time feeling clear, unhindered. The exhaustion-borne hallucinations were gone.

After getting myself together—showering, eating, taking my anti-convulsives—I looked out the window, felt the cool breeze, and saw the bright sunlight. I picked up the phone and called out from work, which is something I never did. Gave no excuses, didn't pretend to be sick. Simply told them that I wasn't coming in that day. Then I called Morgan, who, as it happened, also had a free day in front of her.

After hanging up, I cleaned the apartment a little bit. Set some more food down for the beasts. Then I put on my shoes and hat, checked my pockets to make sure I had my wallet, my keys, and some tokens, and headed for the subway.

Twenty minutes later, a train pulled into the station. The doors opened, and Morgan leaned out, waving. I shuffled for the open door, grabbed her outstretched hand, and she led me to a seat. The doors closed again, and the train pulled out of the station.

Forty-five minutes later, it pulled into an above-ground stop I recognized, even though I could never remember the name.

"This is us," I said.

"You sure?"

"Pretty sure." It had been a while since I'd been down there, and in that time, my eyes had grown much weaker. Perhaps I just smelled that it was our stop.

We got off the train and began following the small crowd that had also stepped off. Down two short flights of steps, through the turnstiles, and back out into sunlight again.

Morgan started guiding me across the arched footbridge that leads to the New York Aquarium, but I stopped her. I didn't want to go to the aquarium. Perfectly nice aquarium and all, but I didn't care to go there right then. Instead, I led her down a ramp that dumped us out on Surf Avenue, at the beginning of the long stretch of Russian junk shops. They looked the same as they always did.

Across the street, the Cyclone stood silent against the sky.

We walked along Surf to the building that housed the indoor carousel. The calliope music was blaring, but the horses were still. A few blocks farther down the street was the original Nathan's hot-dog stand, that famous old green neon sign still hanging over the sidewalk.

We crossed the street, and I started leading her down the same empty road I had walked two days after my arrival in New York.

Much had changed. Bobby Reynolds' Two-Headed Baby and Hundred Pound Rat! exhibits were gone, maybe just for the season, maybe for good. I didn't know, but I found myself hoping that the do-gooders hadn't shut them down, the way they've shut down so many other worthwhile things in this world. The newer hipster sideshow was there, and though it was open, we passed on by. We'd seen it a few times, and, unlike the two-headed baby, it had very quickly lost its novelty.

"Midget," Morgan whispered to me, giving my sleeve a slight tug.

I squinted, and sure enough, a few yards in front of us, a black midget wearing overalls was strolling down the sidewalk on bowed legs. He paused, waved, and called to some people across the street, then crossed to meet them.

"It's good luck if a black midget crosses your path," I noted.

The chain-link fences were still there, as were the giant bumblebees. They'd been given a fresh coat of paint and were polished up nice. They gleamed in the sunlight.

I gave Morgan's hand a little squeeze, and we kept moving. I wanted to check on the entrance to Hell—which had for years been disguised as the Hell Hole ride.

When we first stopped in front of the building and I began to scan the paint job, everything seemed to be in order. It had been repainted again. There were more blues and grays than blacks and reds this time, and less fire. But plenty of monsters, it looked like.

"The Ghost 'Hole'?" Morgan asked.

"No, no—it's the Hell Hole."

"Up there it says 'Ghost Hole.'"

My eyes drifted upward, and sure enough, where the name was painted across the top in enormous letters, it read GHOST HOLE.

Well, that's stupid, I thought. *It doesn't even make any sense.* "They probably had to change the name after that woman got mangled in here a few years ago. I mean, the ride was called the "Hell Hole," for godsake—what did she expect? Her own damn fault."

It wasn't just the name that had changed. The 𝔄bandon 𝔄ll 𝔥ope sign was gone from above the doorway. Worse, the old demon gargoyle who used to perch up there was gone as well. Granted, some sort of winged Hydra creature had replaced him, it might have even been King Ghidorah, but it just wasn't the same. Not to me, at least.

"It's still pretty creepy," Morgan said.

"Oh," I sighed, "but it's just not the same. Unless they're trying to disguise it—make people think it's *not* really, y'know, the gateway to Hell. Grab more souls that way. If that's the case, then it's fine by me."

"You have to admit the demon up there's awfully good," she observed.

I glanced up and sighed again, still very happy to be here in spite of it, and we moved on toward the Boardwalk.

As with that first time, the season had ended a few weeks earlier, so almost everything was closed. The gates were down and the fences were locked. All the rides—the Cyclone, the Wonder Wheel—remained still and silent, except for the wind whistling through their trellises.

"You want something to eat?"

"What do you suppose'll be open?"

"A few places should be, still. We'll be able to get a hot dog, corn dog. Something fried."

"I could use a beer," she said.

"Me, too." I looked at my watch. Eleven-thirty in the morning. I was worried for a moment that we might be too early. Most bars in the city didn't open until one or later. But after we had strolled a mere few yards down the uncluttered and uncrowded Boardwalk, it was clear that we had nothing to worry about. I should have known that different rules governed Coney.

Next to the man selling hot dogs and corn dogs, fried clams, and several other unidentifiable fried objects from inside a glass case sat Ruby's, the eternal Coney tavern. Better still, they were serving. Open-fronted, cement-floored, its walls covered with hundreds of framed black-and-white photographs, each one a frozen moment from Coney's past century. Luna Park after the fire. A large woman in a black bathing suit lying in the snow on the beach. The Mermaid Parade.

At the bar sat several old men and one woman, in the sunshine, by the ocean, beers in hands at eleven-thirty, hot-dog stand not ten feet away.

I'd been to Ruby's before, certainly. In fact, last time I was there, I was there with Morgan. But it wasn't until now that it became so patently obvious that Ruby's Bar was the bar of my dreams. The gates of Heaven so close to the gates of Hell. It only made sense.

I bought Morgan a hot dog and got a corn dog for myself. Most of the seats at the bar being filled already, we sat down at one of the dozen small scarred tables, and Morgan bought us a couple of bottles.

Just then, the jukebox next to us abruptly screamed into life.

"*Come ona my house to my-y house . . .*"

We both smiled, and drank.

For no particular reason, my mind drifted back momentarily to the book party and my hands around that soft neck.

I'm not a tough guy anymore. Far from it. For an old, tired blind man, though, I think I did okay that night. Maybe Grandpa Roscoe was still in there someplace. Quieter, maybe, but still hanging around, and I was glad.

The one thing that frightened me a little bit after trying to strangle that kid to death was recognizing how damned *good* it felt. Sometimes the High Road sucks, simple as that. More than sucks, actually. Sometimes the High Road is a false and useless and dangerous path. Not always, not even usually, but sometimes. And sometimes, in order to feel again, in order to be human again, a man has to reintroduce himself to the animal inside. What we call the primal, negative emotions are good and necessary things when put to proper use. They're quite handy at times for perspective and comparison, and at others for entertainment value. There were things I continued to feel remorse over, acts of violence and cruelty, but that scene at the book party wasn't one of them.

Lord knows I wasn't exactly Hemingway. I wasn't out there taunting elephants and punching out swordfish or any such thing. But it was something. It was almost like the old days again. Except that this time, as with my Grandpa Roscoe, I'd had a reason for my actions, and a good one.

Hemingway was a writer I never came to appreciate until I was older. Much older, perhaps, than I should've been. In fact, it wasn't until the simple pleasure of reading was almost beyond me, when I was forced to listen to Hemingway on audiotape (read by such Papa-esque characters as Charlton Heston, Brian Dennehy, or the great Stacy Keach), that it finally began to hit home.

In his short story "Fathers and Sons," a passage in which Nick Adams describes his father stuck with me:

Then, too, he was sentimental, and like most sentimental people, he was both cruel and abused. Also, he had much bad luck, and it was not all of it his own. He had died in a trap that he had helped only a little to set, and they had all betrayed him in their various ways before he died. All sentimental people are betrayed so many times.

Was "sentimental" even the right word for what I'd become? I didn't think so. While *Dodes ka-den, Night of the Hunter,* Act III of *Parsifal,* and Stan Rogers records had always made me cry, I still preferred angry writers and cruel movies. Moreover, I didn't feel particularly "betrayed" by anyone or anything except myself and my body. Not for a while, anyway—and even before that, only in a very few specific and clear instances.

So that wasn't it, but something had happened. I thought back to my reaction to those kids on the train. That weary, grumpy-old-man disdain that sometimes arises when you recognize too much of yourself, or what you feel you might have left behind, in a younger generation.

I initially put it down to little more than "maturing," or "growing up," but that struck me as too cheap an excuse, especially when so much of what I did and thought remained decidedly immature. Far more than that, I attributed it to getting old and slowing down. Even in my early thirties, my body couldn't do the things it used to do anymore—partly, at least, as a direct result of those things I *had* done before.

Another possible explanation was simply the Tegretol, the anti-convulsive medication I took every day to keep the seizures under control. Recent studies had shown that Tegretol was also very effective as a mood stabilizer, and as a result, useful on manic-depressives. That, too, would be too easy an explanation of why I no longer found myself suffocating under regular suicidal depressions or exploding with hatred at everything I saw (or didn't see). I certainly wasn't a fucking ray of sunshine all the time. Christ, if you don't get really pissed now and again, you're simply not human. Even as I did erupt, however, I noticed that it rarely had the savage quality it had once had. Again I worried that maybe I was simply repressing it all, and that some day soon I'd have an entire army of murderous dwarves out there doing my evil bidding (which, admittedly, would be pretty cool).

It simply didn't feel, stopping to think about it, like I was repressing anything. Even all those unholy lumps and pustules that had once cluttered the left half of my body had faded and eventually vanished on their own accord. The eyeball on my ankle shrank away to nothing without any medical assistance. Sure, things would creep out of me now and again—a facial twitch or a flash of rage—but I could more often than not put it down as the result of being drunk or tired or sweaty.

A better explanation might be that with experience, I'd come to realize that most things we encounter on a daily basis, both good and bad, are tenuous and ephemeral and simply not worth getting all that worked up about. The world is full of small, unchangeable annoyances that simply aren't deserving

216

of all the aggravation they seem to cause in so many. If they are indeed un-changeable annoyances, it's best either to deal with them or ignore them, whether it be blindness or subways that get overcrowded during rush hour. The blindness ain't going away, so it's best to learn to function around it.

That doesn't stop people from stomping around the city in a perpetual fury—people for whom everything leads to a shrill, frothing tantrum, for whom everything's an injustice. *Well*, I can't help but think, *no it's not.* Some things just happen. *Most* things just happen, in fact. And most things that seem to be unjust are more often than not the result of simple, inescapable human stupidity. And what in the hell are you going to do about that?

The thing I've found about those perpetually angry people is that, al-though they can be awfully funny for a while, what with their twitchy angry ways, they get really boring in short order.

(Except for Louis-Ferdinand Céline. He was spewing bile to the end, and God bless him for it.)

I looked at people—regular people, those accidental faces on the sidewalk, in stores, on trains, and in bars. People whose lives seemed to be rolling along fairly smoothly. People who seemed, many of them, to at least be comfort-able. Many of them are very nice, simple, kind people. They mind their own business and are happy to remain invisible. They deal with their own prob-lems in their own way and avoid inflicting them upon everyone around them.

But too many of the people I encountered, it struck me, were assholes. Needlessly so. Consciously or unconsciously, they seemed to go to great lengths to make sure that the lives of everyone they met became a little less pleasant. Worse, they do this in the most unimaginative ways possible. They badgered hapless waitresses and store clerks. They screamed into cell phones, shoved their way onto subway cars, and butted into lines. They inflicted their distemper-ridden children on otherwise-peaceable taverns and clogged the sidewalks with their slow-moving double strollers. All of them minor infractions, perhaps, but they really started to get to me. It wasn't just a symptom of New York, either. If anything, New Yorkers in general turned out to be much more affable and polite than even they would have you believe. No, the assholes are everywhere, and I wondered why.

So many of us spend time most every day ruining things for other people, in ways that range from the mild to the extravagant. Stepping on feet, letting a door slam in someone's face, accepting credit for work someone else has done, stealing from the handicapped, cleaning a loaded gun at the kitchen table, herding all the hostages into the back room, releasing something into the atmosphere that takes hundreds of lives.

Some of these acts may seem insignificant at the time, but even the forgotten ones linger, building on one another, eating away at the spirit, and leading to grandiose, heavy-duty resentment, and sometimes worse. Unfortunately, we rarely stop to give this a second thought.

I was well aware of the fact that I had been a very conscious, almost fanatical asshole up to a point just a few years earlier, but I tried not to be that way anymore.

Once my body started falling to pieces (especially the eyes and the brain), my basic, operative philosophy, if you can call it that, became "Deal with it." I didn't want to be a whiner, another professional victim. There were too many victims around as it was, and I didn't care for them. It wasn't even a conscious decision on my part—it was simply never an issue. It was the way I was raised. If things don't go your way, well, deal with it.

While that was certainly still the case, there was another bit of low-rent, half-assed psycho philosophy that I'd tacked on behind it somewhere along the line—sort of a corollary to "Deal with it"—namely, "Don't be a shit."

That doesn't mean I became some namby-pamby little Candide with a smile in my heart and a kind word for even the lowliest vermin. Hardly. But choosing not to be a shit just made sense. Even in the most selfish of terms it made sense. You want to get good service in a store, in a restaurant, or while dealing with a government agency? Then don't be a shit. Remember that in most cases, the people you're dealing with are under just as much stress and have just as many unspoken crises facing them as you do, so show a little patience—and tip well. In my situation at the newspaper, if I wanted, say, someone from the NYPD to tell me about a case, I'd discovered that if I was pleasant to them and asked politely, they'd tell me all I wanted to know and more (plus it would be accurate). If I took the attitude of some pugnacious twat, they'd never tell me a thing, and I'd be stuck.

The more you try it, the easier it is to do. Most of us have troubles enough as it is, and it simply makes things a little easier. Don't be a shit, and more often than not, you'll get the same in return. Not always, of course, but, as William Burroughs noted, some people are just shits.

It sounds so basic and banal, but so few people do it, and they end up leaving any situation with more things to complain about, more lives to make miserable, and more ammunition with which to bore the rest of us.

I'm sure there are much more eloquent, profound ways to express it, but "Don't be a shit" says it well enough for me.

To put it another way, if you're a shit, you go through life assuming everyone else is a shit, too. That's the way I was, at least. If you're thinking and acting that way, you'll always be proven right.

If, however, you aren't a shit, you realize that while yeah, sure, there are plenty of shits out there, there are plenty of non-shits as well. What's more, you realize that most of the shits can be laughed off.

If that makes any sense.

At the same time, there's no denying that we need our shits around, like we do our negative emotions, for perspective's sake and entertainment value. I harbor the deepest respect, and at times envy, for bank robbers and other outlaws. They're people who, as I once tried, embodied the very nature of chance: Dillinger, Capone, The Mentors' El Duce, Willie Sutton, Jerry Lee Lewis, Jack Black (the author, not the actor), hundreds of others. They were criminals, they were outlaws, they were, in that way, professional shits. But professional shits with style, class, talent, and guts. They had their own codes, their own rules, and they lived by them, becoming almost mythical in the process.

Of course Grinch's name is on that list, too. Up there with the best of them. Despite his worldly success, his heart was still as black as tar, and I respected that.

Grinch somehow (and perhaps this should worry me) seemed to have had some sort of direct connection with several major disasters that made the news over the past quarter-century, beginning with the Three Mile Island mishap. So it was no surprise that I received a note from him the day after a third-floor porch in the Lincoln Park section of Chicago collapsed during a party, killing a dozen college students:

Jim,

  Let me get you caught up on what I've been up to lately

  1. I went on an extended business trip through Sicily & Southern Italy.

  2. For the first time in over twenty years, I enjoyed a dramatic and thorough paranoiac breakdown. Think Céline's Bardamu on the ship to Africa, and put it on a bus going around Italy, and that's pretty much what happened to me.

  3. I sold my house in only three weeks. My new house still isn't ready. I was forced to move my family into a dilapidated studenty apartment in Lincoln Park for the interim.

  4. The night after I moved in, the whiteboys next door were having a noisy kegger party out on the third-floor stoop. Shortly before 12:30 AM, the stairway they were hanging out on collapsed, squashing all the hapless fools that were partying on the second-floor landing. Thirteen down, six billion to go!

   ASK NOT FOR WHOM THE HOLE SMELLS!
Grinch

My first reaction upon reading the note wasn't concern over the breakdown he mentioned. No, the first, immediate, gut reaction was *"I wonder how he managed to rig that porch collapse?"* For some reason, I wouldn't have been surprised at all.

Most of the shits we encounter aren't as flashy or charismatic as the ones mentioned above. Most are little more than petty, snide, and rude, with nothing behind it, no justification, no style, no reason for being that way. And most are incredibly stupid.

Those early years, when my assholery and shititude were rampant, were years in which I had nothing. No job, no hope, and the rent was always pretty iffy. I was struggling, I was clawing to get anything at all—I was starving, I was drinking out of bitterness, and I was paying no consideration whatsoever to anyone else around me. Given my circumstances, I concluded that I would never get anywhere. As a result, I destroyed things (both physically and in newsprint) that belonged to other people. I was forging a character based on the rage of my youth, which was still carrying me into adulthood. Struggle can make anyone an asshole, if only out of simple desperation. You see all these happy people around you who have so much more than you do, you're going to resent it.

The contradictory thing on my part was the fact that, if asked, I wouldn't have been able to name anything I wanted. I didn't really want anything. I was miserable and desperate and angry, but without any goal in mind. I was just waiting.

Yet at the same time, you look at the people who are seemingly farthest ahead in life—the ones with gobs of money, who are in positions of power and authority—they're almost inevitably assholes. The biggest ones of all, even. My guess is that John Doe was right, and they're greedy. They have a lot and they want more—and that reduces them to that same desperate status as the panhandler looking over the passengers in the train car with bitter eyes, or me, sitting on my living-room floor with a three-dollar bottle of Ecuadorian wine.

In my case, several things started happening in the mid- to late nineties. I fell into a little luck.

The eyes started to go and go much earlier and faster than anyone had expected. My first book came out, and even if it didn't rocket up any bestseller lists, people were very kind to it. I got the staff-writer job and was able to step away from that godforsaken reception desk. As nuts as being a staff writer drove me sometimes (and what job doesn't?) it was a hell of a lot better than sitting inside that white cube any longer. And of course there was

Morgan, whom I met shortly after getting out of a marriage that, in its final years, had been quiet, sad, and without laughter. She showed me that I could still laugh, laugh hard, and laugh at damn near anything.

All of those things, in their own way, from the blindness to the books, forced me, for the first time in a long time, to work with other people, think about other people, even count on the kindness of other people in order to get around. Even though I still preferred isolation and chose it when I could, I'd learned to look at dealing with people as something other than combat.

The act of transferring a book from inside your head to a bookstore shelf, for example, requires that the author work with a small army—editors, copy editors, agents, lawyers, proofreaders, publicists, reviewers, and the like. I found that if you're nice to those people, there will be much more enthusiasm concerning the project all around. I guess that's true in any working relationship.

I suddenly needed to accept the help of others, which was something I had been hesitant—had even refused—to do before. I started listening to voices other than my own (not all of them in my head) and I realized that they weren't all out to get me. They'd help me across the street if I needed it, and they wouldn't ask me for anything in return. Not most of them, anyway.

Over the years, I was also lucky enough to encounter a number of people who weren't shits, and who would become friends (even as I continued to hide most of the time). They were wise and talented, and extremely intelligent. Yet they seemed to be at peace, in a way, probably because they knew they had nothing to prove to anyone. They were kind; they were, in a word, good.

I thought of all these other people, too, all the voices—from Harry Crews to the Ratcatcher—handing me the little pieces of wisdom along the way that I finally started paying attention to.

Other people don't need boots in the ass like that in order to come to their senses, but I'd been so consciously awful for so long (and was certainly far enough from perfect now) that I guess I did.

My parents had raised me well. They treated others and me and themselves with simple kindness and respect. I'd rejected that, but now, slowly, it was making all the sense in the world.

It wasn't an abrupt change. There were no flashes of lightning, no enormous, life-altering revelations. It happened slowly and quietly. So slowly and quietly, in fact, that I didn't even notice it had happened until some time later. It had just happened, is all.

In my case, the goals weren't all that lofty. I achieved more than I ever thought I would in life, given circumstances and abilities, and I did so quite by accident. Even if I always hoped I'd be better at any number of things, the fact that any of it happened at all is much more than I ever could have expected.

It took a long damn time and, accidental or not, it took a lot of work, but there was no need to struggle anymore, no need to scramble and scratch. There was nothing I felt I needed to prove anymore, and so there was no need to be a shit to everyone.

I still can be a shit, of course. We all can, but that's human. I bet even that Gandhi fellow was a shit now and again. I try not to be, but in small, unconscious ways it still comes out without my even noticing. I still have my black moods, I still get unduly frustrated when I get stuck in a line that's not going anywhere, and I still unconsciously fall into my Germanic schedules. I'm still irrationally fearful of most plants and of men wielding garden hoses. In general, though, if everything's okay, why fight it?

I'm certainly less spastic and frantic than I used to be. I worry about fewer things. Why bother with it? Things pass. Things resolve themselves. I still puke before I'm scheduled to do a reading, but in the end I do it, get it over with, and it's gone. Everything passes. Everything except memory, that is—and even memory decays with time.

There are problems with this, of course—with trying to be pleasant and in accepting the random nature of things. Contradictions are inevitable.

If you let things roll off of you too easily, if you don't get all hepped up about much of anything, sometimes you can find yourself accepting a situation that is less than ideal, even if it could very easily be changed. It could be something as simple as sweating through another unbearable summer because buying a new air conditioner seems like too much of a pain in the ass, or bringing a nest of bedbugs into work with you every day. You could find yourself placated and sedate with awful jobs or awful relationships or in letting people walk all over you. If you take acceptance to an extreme, then you're nothing more than some spineless, uninteresting slug.

226

Acceptance is one thing, I guess, so long as you're not stupid about it. Dream, yes, always—it's those dreams and the risks we take to realize them that end up taking us places. So dream, but be open to things. Try to do what you want, but accept that it won't always work out the way you planned. When it doesn't, deal.

It occurs to me that everything I'm trying to say here, as clunky and incoherent as it is, can be found in Rudyard Kipling's poem "If," stated in a much more elegant manner. He even makes it rhyme. (Or, if you think the Kipling is too overworked, just watch a Douglas Cheek movie. Most of the answers to life's puzzles, I've discovered, can be found in Douglas Cheek movies.)

I got lucky along the way, and I know I got lucky. For now. I also know that there are plenty of people for whom things haven't worked out at all. Their husbands or wives have left them with nothing. They're stuck in miserable, humiliating jobs. They have children in hopeless situations who need impossible medical care. They're in prison for a crime they didn't commit. They're diagnosed with incurable diseases. Worse circumstances than most of us could ever realize. Bringing up any of these things is hardly a comfort to someone in a situation like that. Sometimes, however, sadly, that's all we've got.

In the end, maybe part of accepting things includes accepting our own contradictions and failures. We're human, after all, the most fallible of creatures, and our lives aren't lived in terms of the rules laid out by the philosophers and theologians. The things that happen to us don't always make sense. We're not rational. We don't think or act rationally. Most of the time we just make it up as we go along, best we can.

I've rarely acted rationally myself, lord knows, but I don't regret any of the turns I've made along the way. I don't look back and wish that any of those coin tosses had come up heads instead of tails, that any of those dice rolls had come up five instead of snake eyes (except maybe in the case of that adult-diaper commercial). In the end, they were, all of them, necessary. Even some of the things I regret now were necessary.

I don't want any of this to sound like that touchy-feely, new-agey "You Are the Miracle" crap. For the record, some of the ugliest, nastiest, most unpleasant people I've had the misfortune of dealing with are new-agey self-help gurus. They're among the biggest shits of them all.

No, instead I prefer to think of all this more as "Buddhism for Drunkards." I'm not telling anyone what to do or how to be. All I can do is describe my own experience. In the end, that's pretty much all any of us can do. And in my case, things right now are okay.

Or maybe it is just the Tegretol talking.

Morgan and I sat at that scarred table in Ruby's for about an hour, listening to the jukebox and ordering another beer. Some of the people who'd been sitting at the bar when we first arrived were starting to leave.

There was a cool salt breeze off the Atlantic. After we were finished with that second round, Morgan asked, "Can we go down to the water?"

"'Course. Let's go." I took her arm.

The bartender—a tall man with graying hair and a salt-and-pepper mustache—waved and smiled at us as we left.

Different rules altogether, I thought.

We crossed the Boardwalk to the short flight of steps that led down to the sand. Morgan stopped and removed her shoes and socks. I left mine on.

"Aren't you going to take your shoes off?"

"Naaah, I'll be fine."

"You sure? They'll get all full of sand."

"I'm okay. I don't care."

We walked across the warm sand, Morgan keeping her eyes open for broken glass and stray hypodermic needles, but much to our amazement, the beach was pristine. Soft, smooth, almost completely free of garbage.

A few scattered sunbathers were spread out closer to the water. Most of them were in their fifties or older, the men unself-consciously letting their huge bellies flop over the fronts of their trunks. There was a time when such a thing, for some reason, would have terrified me, but now it struck me as a strange, epic form of grace. They were beyond caring, they were satisfied without arrogance. They didn't give a good goddamn what people thought. They were comfortable.

A man in a small, unmotorized dune buggy sped along the shore, propelling himself by means of a giant kite, which he controlled with two aluminum sticks.

There was nothing to block the sun—no clouds, no trees or buildings—but the direct heat was tempered by the ocean breeze.

We reached the edge of the water, and I continued to move forward until Morgan stopped me. "Baby—your shoes are going to get all wet."

"I don't care. C'mon." I urged her farther.

"But you'll spend the rest of the day in soggy socks."

"I don't care. C'mon." The first wave crashed across our ankles.

"Jesus, baby," she pleaded. "C'mon. Please. Just take your damn shoes off."

I shrugged, walked back out to the dry sand, squatted down, and removed my shoes and socks. Standing again, I felt warm sand beneath my feet for the first time in, what? Thinking back, it had been at least twenty years. I guess in that time, I'd never much been in the mood.

We stepped toward the water again, and my pant legs from the knees down were soon soaked. I removed my hat, as the Atlantic had stolen more than one of my hats in the past. We began to walk up the beach toward Brighton, the Russian neighborhood just up the coast from Coney, stopping occasionally as Morgan pointed out various forms of sea and beach life. The crashing waves washed across our feet.

A man who was either insane or drunk stumbled past us, muttering dark thoughts to himself and smiling. He was wearing a black suit. Ancient joggers hobbled past us with tiny, insistent steps. The guy in the kite-propelled dune buggy sped this way and that, not running anybody over, much to our surprise.

As I tried to keep the clinging tendrils of my too-long hair out of my face (impossible without the hat), Morgan began to point out tiny crab parts scattered across the sand. Legs and claws, mostly, and a few empty shells.

In the water, the seagulls bobbed idly, riding the waves, uninterested and unhurried. As we watched one floating near an outcropping of rocks, it ducked its head beneath the water and came back up with a live crab in its beak. It shook it slightly, then dropped it. Dove again and retrieved it.

"I wonder how they eat them?" she asked.

The gull, crab now firmly in beak, paddled the few yards to shore, stepped onto the sand, then shook the crab violently, sending tiny claws and spidery legs free in every direction. It dropped the now-legless mass of the crab's body onto the beach, paused a moment, then savagely drove its beak through the shell.

"I, ummm . . . I think you have your answer there," I observed.

We continued to watch from a few short feet away as the gull quickly ripped the crab to pieces, pecking small bits of meat from within the broken shell and the scattered claws.

"Those damn crabs sure aren't put together too well, it seems," I noted. "Those legs came right the hell off."

Other gulls joined in the frenzy, and we continued up the beach for a few hundred yards more before turning and walking in the other direction, back the way we'd come, the ocean water cooling my scarred feet and soaking my pants.

"You should've rolled those up," Morgan said. She knew I didn't own a pair of shorts.

"Yeah, probably would've been the thing to do. But there you go."

On our way back down the beach, we watched more gulls kill and dismember more crabs. The dune buggy scooted past us another half-dozen times. Then we stopped, and I squeezed her shoulders.

"How ya doin'?" I asked.

She smiled. "I'm very happy."

"Yeah? Me, too . . . I love you."

"I love you, too."

I looked out over the clean, empty sand, and all the dark, empty water that would someday carry my ashes away. I knew then that if I died that night—if a train ran over me, or a passing bicyclist with a gun took me out, or the cats sucked my breath away as I slept, or I somehow impaled myself on my own cane—hell, even if I died before that—if that guy with the dune buggy clipped me a good one, or if the waters of the Atlantic suddenly rose up to bury Brooklyn the way the waters of the Red River had buried Grand Forks, or if those long-expected flashpots went off under my feet as I stood there on the beach—in short, if my ashes were going to end up drifting off the pier within a week's time, I could still close my dim eyes, safe and content with the knowledge that, yeah, broken and weakened as I was, things were okay, really.

If there's one thing that all these clogged and sputtering and often-burdensome memories of mine have taught me, it's that life simply happens. It's not a profound lesson, but it's a true one. Try as we might to control it, gauge it, order it, tie it up, and point it in the right direction, we'll never succeed. Something will always come along to knock it off the tracks, for better or for worse. One of your children dies, the company you work for goes under, a beverage vehicle sideswipes you while doing sixty, a meteor hits the house, you go blind. Or the right person finally comes along, or the right job, or the tornado skips your place. You lose the feeling in your legs one morning. The numbers come up in your favor. You go mad. You kill a man in an unthinking rage. That little fire gets out of hand. On a whim you put your money on a hundred-to-one shot. You change your mind after ten years. Or forty-one years.

All of these things can happen, have happened, will continue to happen, for no reason at all or for the best reasons in the world. A lot of hair-pulling and jumping about. Looking back on it, it was so simple to see. It just happened, that's all. A bunch of things. And here we are. We do terrible things, we do kind things—and sometimes one side far outweighs the other. Sometimes they balance each other out quite nicely.

The things we do here, the smallest things, really do matter, not because of any eternal rewards or punishments that might be awaiting us, but rather because they're all we've got. While we're here, the shattered days as well as the glorious ones add up. While we're here, they mean something—like this moment, with my gal on the beach at Coney.

We try and sometimes we fail. By the same token, despite all the terrible mistakes we make, sometimes we succeed, if briefly. Sometimes. And that's okay.

Even if everything around and within me failed again, which no doubt it will in some form, I still had this moment and this day. I could smile comfortably, without shame, like the fat old Russian men who put their proud bellies on public display.

Coney was as close as I came to having a church. It was my Mecca, my Lourdes, and my Wailing Wall. There, with Morgan, it was where hope lay.

"Thirsty?" I asked.

"Sure am," she said, and smiled again.

We headed back across the warm sand to the Boardwalk, where we stopped and put our shoes back on. A group of Asian teenage boys stopped to remove their own shoes, then ran whooping toward the water.

We went back into Ruby's and sat down at the now mostly empty bar. On the jukebox, Dean Martin was singing a song that was all too appropriate. The bartender grinned at us as he approached and said, "I knew you'd be back. Two again?"

We both nodded, and I lit another cigarette as he went to retrieve them from the cooler at the other end of the bar.

When the beers arrived, I laid a couple of bills beneath the ashtray, put my hand on Morgan's knee and gave it a light squeeze, and we clinked bottles.

"Cheers, baby."

acknowledgments

The author wishes to humbly thank the following people for their continued encouragement and patience, as well as their steady supply of bad jokes:

Ken Siman; David Groff; Sara Carder; Stuart Calderwood; Mom and Dad; Mary, Bob, McKenzie, and Jordan; John Strausbaugh, Lisa Kearns, Sam Sifton, Jeff Koyen, Alex Zaitchik, and most of the rest of the *New York Press* staff both past and present; Derek Davis; Ken Swezey and Laura Lindgren; Innes Smolansky; Melanie Jackson; Marty Asher; Homer Flynn; Bill Monahan; Scott Ferguson; Russell Christian; Gary Hertz; TRP; Don Kennison; Paul Rickert; Mike Walsh; David E. Williams; Dave and Sarah Read; d.b.a.; Ruby's; Bill Lustig; Flo Schultheiss; Murray Cockerill (he once was lost, but now is found); and the great Fats Waller and Ennio Morricone, for providing the soundtrack.

Jim Knipfel lives in Brooklyn, where he doesn't bother anybody much.